PRAISE FOR
THE POWER OF ONE

"My friend, Dr. Billy Wilson, is one of the most gifted visionary leaders I have ever known. His passion to reach everyone in the world, one person at a time, is both inspiring and infectious. I highly recommend *The Power of One* to every believer and leader. You will be inspired to join a global movement to complete the Great Commission in our generation, a movement that Billy is helping spearhead."

– Brian Alarid
President of World Prays and Chairman of Pray For All

"If every believer would reach the 'ones' around them, we would have an overnight spiritual awakening! If every believer would set their eyes on the 'ones' all over the world who have no Gospel access, we could finish the Great Commission! Dr. Wilson is not only leading this charge, he has given us this book as a timely, prophetic, and visionary charge for the incredible hour we live in! Let us take up this cause together to reach the 'one.'"

– Andy Byrd
YWAM Kona, The Send

"Dr. Wilson reminds us that all people matter to God; all people have the ability to respond to the message of salvation; and all people can fulfill their God-given potential. *The Power of One* is a call to move beyond missiological thinking into missiological action and is a reminder that finishing the Great Commission is doable!"

– Doug Clay
General Superintendent, Assemblies of God

"There is a big risk with individualism if it starts and ends with the person's ego. But when there is a commitment to take personal responsibility to reach yet another person with the gospel, the whole world can be changed. When many decide to connect with just one person, the Church is on the move! This is an important document from Dr. Wilson, and it is filled with the Pentecostal passion that characterizes his ministry. May we all live in a Decade of Revival bringing in a great harvest!"

– Daniel Alm
General Superintendent, Swedish Pentecostal Movement

"Perhaps the most serious mandate Christ placed upon us is finishing the Great Commission. As Evangelical and Charismatic believers, we have the greatest and most effective set of soul-winning tools at our disposal. Billy Wilson is one of the most skilled craftsmen at using those tools when it comes to reaping the harvest. In *The Power of One,* Dr. Wilson shares his experiences, research, and knowledge, but most importantly, his heart for reaching every person on Earth with the Gospel message by 2033."

– Tim Hill
Church of God Presiding Bishop/General Overseer, Cleveland, Tennessee

"*The Power of One,* by Dr. Billy Wilson, is a remarkable book that demonstrates the transformative impact of the gospel and the potential within each believer. It challenges believers to take personal responsibility for the Great Commission, highlighting the opportunities in our interconnected world. Dr. Wilson emphasizes unity within the body of Christ, rooted in love and a common mission. The book inspires readers to bring about spiritual awakenings and a global outpouring of the Holy Spirit, while encouraging active participation in reaching everyone with the message of Jesus Christ. In a broken world, *The Power of One* is a timely guide for faith, unity, and personal responsibility, leaving readers inspired and ready to make an impact. It is a must-read for those seeking transformation in their lives and communities."

– Terry Parkman

Empowered21 NextGen Global Co-Chair, NextGen Pastor, River Valley Church, OneHope Global NextGen Ambassador

"The first time I met Dr. Wilson, I discovered a brilliant and anointed man carrying God's heart in such a unique way. A few years later, when he shared the 'EveryONE' initiative, I started to cry as I was hearing and feeling Jesus' deep heart and urgent desire to save every single soul. This book is a holy-massive-glorious bomb that displays a major key for believers of this new era to fulfill and to finish the Great Commission. As 'each one' of us stops for the 'one' and reaches 'someone' with the Gospel, very soon EVERYONE on this Earth will hear the Good News, and for the first time in history, we will be able to see with our own eyes an entire generation saved before the coming of our Lord Jesus Christ. Hallelujah! This generation shall be saved!"

– Jean-Luc Trachsel

President of the International Association of Healing Ministries (IAHM), President and founder of Europe Shall Be Saved (ESBS), Member of the Apostolic Team, Gospel Wave in Switzerland, Empowered21 Global Evangelist Alliance (GEA) Co-Chair

"The impact of personal evangelism has been at the heart of soul winning since the inception of sharing the gospel. In his book, *The Power of One,* Dr. Billy Wilson has once again illuminated the value of each person's individual influence in saving the lost. Reflecting on a personal encounter with God that resulted in a refreshed and expanded vision, he takes the reader on a journey that is simple yet profound. Whether a new or seasoned Christian, each will be challenged to do more!"

– Dr. Tony D. Stewart
Assistant General Overseer, Church of God

"If our culture has shown us anything in recent years, it presents to us a world in desperate need of the good news of Jesus. In *The Power of One,* Dr. Billy Wilson offers both the challenge before us and the remarkable opportunity to proclaim the gospel in the power of the Spirit. As president of Oral Roberts University, I particularly appreciate his insight into Gen Z and its potential as a gospel force. We need a fresh burden for the lost and a renewed practice of evangelism that this book details!"

– Dr. Ed Stetzer
Dean of Talbot School of Theology

"Change starts with one man or woman saying, 'Yes.' Many hearts are being ignited in the Body of Christ for each member to play their part in a new era of soul-winning. *In The Power of One*, Dr. Wilson masterfully takes us through the biblical examples of how one interaction changed the course of history. With urgency in the pages, this book activates every believer to stand in this hour to declare that 'Jesus Christ is Lord.' This book will both challenge and inspire you to make your 'Yes' count for eternity."

– Nathan Morris

Founder and President, Shake The Nations Ministries

In *The Power of One*, my mentor and friend, Dr. Billy Wilson, issues a clarion call for the purpose of activating the "one." One person set free in the name of Jesus can change a generation. A multitude of "ones" filled with the power of the Holy Spirit can literally change the world. This book reminds all of us to be the "one" that reaches the "one" for the purpose of worshiping the "One"—Jesus, the risen Christ.

—Rev. Samuel Rodriguez

Lead Pastor, New Season Church, President and CEO of NHCLC

"My heart always burns when I talk about finishing the Great Commission of the Lord Jesus. That is why my heart is very happy to know that *The Power of One* is published. This book clearly explains the importance of one person to reach everyONE in sharing the Good News of Salvation. I believe that after reading this book, every person will be moved by their heart to immediately finish the Great Commission. By 2033, everyONE will have an authentic encounter with the Lord Jesus."

– Pastor Niko Njotorahardjo
Senior Pastor, Gereja Bethel Indonesia

"The Power of One, by Dr. Wilson, is a must-read for anyone who desires to make a lasting impact for the cause of Christ. In this book, Dr. Wilson shares his expertise and insight on how to effectively reach people with the gospel of Jesus Christ. His approach is practical, easy to understand, and biblically grounded.

"Dr. Wilson's passion for sharing the gospel is contagious, and his writing style is engaging and easy to follow. This book is packed with wisdom and practical advice that will inspire and equip readers to make a difference in the lives of those around them.

"If you are looking for a book that will challenge you to step out of your comfort zone and share the love of Christ with others, *The Power of One* is the book for you. I highly recommend it!"

– Reggie Dabbs
The Youth Alliance

"Dr. Billy Wilson has continually maintained his pulse on what God is doing on Earth and what He is doing in the next generation. In *The Power of One,* you will be challenged to your core to step off the sidelines to reach someONE with the Gospel. In an era of tribalism and divisive belief systems, the time to unite to see a world reached is now. Whoever you are, wherever you are, join this clarion call to step out and see the world reached in our generation!"

– Eli Bonilla Jr.

Empowered21 NextGen North America Co-Chair, Author of Mixed: Embracing Complexity by Uncovering Your God-led Identity, National NextGen Director, NHCLC

"*The Power of One,* written by Dr. Wilson, is an inspiring and compelling book that calls all Christians globally to unite around one cause, to preach the gospel to everyone, everywhere, over the next decade through the power of the Holy Spirit. We are living in a kairos and pivotal moment in history, and *The Power of One* will ignite your Godly purpose and potential to be part of this end time harvest. *The Power of One* will propel you to participate in an audacious goal to take the good news of Jesus to the ends of the Earth. There are no limits."

– Daniela Freidzon-McCabe
Pastor and Speaker, King of Kings Church, Empowered21 NextGen Global Co-Chair

"In *The Power of One*, Billy Wilson presents an awe-inspiring vision of the global church's potential to fulfill the Great Commission. Drawing from Scripture, history, and personal experiences, Wilson passionately lays out a plan to reach every individual with the Gospel by 2033. This compelling call to action is imbued with a profound understanding of the power of personal encounters with Jesus. *The Power of One* offers a must-read blueprint for believers yearning to impact the world for the Savior, one person at a time."

– Dr. Wayne Hilsden
Co-Founder of King of Kings Community, Jerusalem, President of FIRM: Fellowship of Israel Related Ministries

"In *The Power of One,* Dr. Billy Wilson shares a message that is so important in the days and times we live in. It is a clarion call to action that is inspirational but also very practical. As I read it, I was personally challenged and encouraged regarding my part in the Great Commission. Dr. Wilson is an outstanding leader and communicator who has impacted the lives of countless individuals. In this book, he lays out a clear strategy for every Christian to play their part in the purpose of God in our generation. I genuinely believe that *The Power of One* is a vital resource in this new era of evangelism and should be on the bookshelf of every follower of Jesus."

– Sharon Witton
Toronto City Church Co-Lead Pastor, Empowered21 NextGen North America Co-Chair

"Dr. Billy Wilson is a global voice whose influence is touching lives worldwide. I have had the honor of working with Dr. Wilson and seeing how the vision for reaching everyone on Earth has developed. In this new book, *The Power of One,* everyone can find their role in advancing the Great Commission, and together we can see God's glory cover the Earth."

– Russell Evans
Global Senior Pastor of Planetshakers Church

"Having known Dr. Wilson for many years, I have witnessed and admired his tireless commitment to serving the next generation of Spirit-empowered leaders. In *The Power of One,* he inspires us all with the profound truth that one changed life has the capacity to unlock a multitude of transformations. He reminds us that each individual, regardless of background or influence, possesses immeasurable worth before God. Dr. Wilson's book relays a compelling call to action as it challenges us to embrace the task of reaching every single person with the transformative power of Jesus by 2033. Dr. Wilson's wisdom, combined with his genuine care for people, shines through on every page, leaving us inspired and equipped to embrace our own role in reaching the world, one person at a time."

– Rob Hoskins
President, OneHope, Inc.

OTHER TITLES BY BILLY WILSON

Father Cry:

Healing Your Heart and the Hearts of Those You Love

Fasting Forward:

Advancing Your Spiritual Life Through Fasting

As the Waters Cover the Sea:

The Story of Empowered21 and the Movement It Serves (co-authored with the late Vinson Synan)

Generation Z:

Born for the Storm

THE
POWER
OF
ONE

BILLY WILSON

Empowered Books
An Imprint of ORU Press
Tulsa, Oklahoma USA

CEDAR GATE
PUBLISHING

The Power of One

ISBN– 978-1-950971–29-9

Empowered Books, an imprint of ORU Press, is a registered trademark of Oral Roberts University Press.

Published by Cedar Gate Publishing

Jacket Design and Composition: Hampton Creative, Tulsa, OK

Edited by Holden Hill

Interior design by Cedar Gate Publishing

ACKNOWLEDGMENTS AND DEDICATION

When one writes a book, they often reflect on their life's journey. This is true of *The Power of One*. Stories and reflections within this text span the entirety of my ministry, from my earliest days as a newlywed to a recent encounter with someone in China. I attribute all of these moments and inspirations to the work of the Holy Spirit in my heart and life. He has been my constant Companion since the age of sixteen, and without Him, I could never have accomplished what the Lord has asked of me. Jesus changed my life! If possible, I would tell every person on Earth about Him. My prayer is that this book will help fulfill that goal as you and thousands of others do all you can to reach every person on Earth for Christ.

I want to express special thanks to several people, including Alyssa Sanders, who coordinates content and research for our Oral Roberts University offices; Max Barroso, whose missionary passion has been an inspiration; Kay Horner, who has edited nearly all of the books I have written–what a saint; Charles G. Scott, who is coordinating schedules and distribution; Johnie Hampton and Hampton

Creative for designing another great cover; Lisa Bowman and Eric Peterson, my right and left hands at ORU; my son, Ashley Wilson, for pushing me over the edge to get this done; Holden Hill with Cedar Gate for working with our offices on this project from beginning to end. Special thanks also to my friend Rick Warren for his kindness and words in the foreword. As always, I must express my heart's gratitude for Lisa, who is not only my other constant companion and faithful wife but my consistent encourager.

I dedicate this volume to the multiplied millions of people who have never had a clear opportunity to encounter Jesus and know Him as their Savior. I pray more unreached people will have that opportunity because of the words on these pages. If just one person comes to know Jesus because of the investment of our time, energy, and personal experiences, all will be worthwhile. Remember, when you become ONE who is found, you are immediately commissioned to be ONE who finds others.

Through God's power and our united effort, we can reach every person on Earth for Jesus Christ and demonstrate *The Power of One*.

CONTENTS

FOREWORD

God never does anything accidentally! He has a good purpose behind everything He creates in the universe.

That means you are not an accident! It also means no other person alive is an accident either. God planned them for His pleasure! He formed them for His family. He created them to be like Christ. He shaped them for service. And He made them for a mission! They are priceless.

There are accidental parents, but no accidental children. There are illegitimate parents, but no illegitimate people. Everyone matters to God.

Your parents may not have planned you, but God did! Every person was made BY God and FOR God, who loves them deeply. Until people understand this fact, life will never make sense!

The fact that every person is valuable, loveable, forgivable, and usable by God is the fundamental truth beneath this outstanding new book by my dear friend, Billy Wilson. Every person matters for three significant reasons: 1) God our Father created them. 2) Jesus the Son died for them. 3) God's Holy Spirit wants to live within them. Every human individual is both infinitely valuable and tragically broken. Both descriptions are true. That is why Jesus made all the effort to come to Earth, suffer, and die to save us. Everybody needs Jesus.

If you want to know how valuable every single person is, regardless of their brokenness and sinfulness, just look at Jesus hanging on the cross. With bleeding, nail-pierced hands and His arms outstretched, Jesus was saying, "THIS is how much I love you! This much! I'd rather die than live without you! I planned you, I made you, and I have loved you every second of your life! And no matter how badly you've messed up your life, I can save you."

There are many good motivations for caring about every person in the world and sharing the Good News with every person in the world, but three of the best motivations are these: We're grateful to God for saving our lives, we recognize the worth of every other life, and we want to bring glory to God by seeing lives saved and transformed.

One of the biggest reasons most Christian believers never share their faith is they don't realize how deeply God wants His lost children found.

Just as Jesus explained that the Good Shepherd leaves ninety-nine sheep safe to go after the one sheep that is lost,

The Power of One explains why and how each of us can do our part in reaching everyONE with the Good News that they matter to God, Christ's died for them, and that He wants them in His family forever!

—Rick Warren

Author of *The Purpose Driven Life*

INTRODUCTION

The carpet was soaked with tears as I lay on my face in a small prayer chapel in Cleveland, Tennessee. God's presence was tangible. The time was between 2:00 a.m. and 4:00 a.m., and I was all alone. The revelation I received that morning more than twenty years ago would dramatically shape and change my life. Ultimately, this significant encounter would inspire the thoughts expressed in this book. Let me explain.

Our church was concluding a forty-day fast, and as the lead pastor of the congregation, I had fully participated during the fast by drinking only juice. This was a wonderful season in my life. My body was skinny, my spirit was broken, and my heart was open to hear the Lord's words. During the last week of the fast, the church established a twenty-four-hour, seven-day prayer chain with someone praying in the prayer chapel every hour of the day throughout the week. My committed hour for prayer was from 2:00 to 3:00 each morning. As a pastor, I thought choosing one of the more difficult hours would be a good example to others.

On this particular morning, my one-hour commitment turned into more than a two-hour, intense, spiritual encounter. Though others usually joined me, I was alone this time.

Somewhere during those two hours, the Holy Spirit visited me, and I found myself facedown, crying out to God for a fresh revival in our generation. His voice interrupted my tear-filled prayer with a promise that would change my perspective and ultimately my world.

I heard the Lord say, "I am going to send a second flood—a *new* flood—like the flood of Noah's day. Only this second flood will be spiritual and not physical. This new flood will not be a flood of retribution and justice but of mercy and love. My Spirit is going to flood the Earth!"

Instantly, I felt impressed to read Habakkuk's prophetic words, "For the earth will be filled with the knowledge of the glory of the Lord as the waters cover the sea" (2:14). *How do the waters cover the sea?* I thought. An answer immediately came: *Completely!* Water covers the sea so completely that no dry places remain.

With my face against the ground in that small prayer room, God revealed to me that this flood would be a new outpouring of the Holy Spirit, and it would reach the whole Earth until there were no spiritually dry places left. In Noah's day, the flood came from two sources: forty days and nights of rain from above and the rupture of underground water sources from below (see Genesis

7–8). This new, 21st-century flood would originate from three sources: a fresh, global outpouring of the Holy Spirit like rain from above; the opening of millions of personal rivers of witness from believers around the world like the rupture of hidden waters from below; and the convergence of spiritual streams and movements uniting to bring a confluence of spiritual power.

I staggered from the prayer room that morning, knowing God had spoken to me but in no way comprehending what the words I heard would mean to my life and leadership journey. It's often said that hindsight is 20/20. After twenty years, I can now see that the Lord would use that early morning encounter to prepare me for a spiritually dynamic future. Within months of lying on the tear-soaked carpet in the prayer room, things began shifting in my life. Through a series of providential and supernatural occurrences, I began to transition from being a pastor and denominational leader to a broader kingdom role of servant and convener.

The Lord would require me to devote myself to living the vision He had given that morning and would change my ministry trajectory forever.

First, I was placed in a strategic role between two denominations to bring evangelistic impact and foster unity. Next, I was drafted by necessity into leading the

2006 Azusa Street Centennial Celebration. After the Azusa celebration, our ministry unified evangelical and Spirit-empowered leaders to form the Awakening America Alliance. Three short years later, we established an initiative that became known as Empowered21 to serve the future of the global Spirit-empowered movement. Eventually, I would be honored to become the fourth president of Oral Roberts University (ORU) and recently was elected to chair the historic Pentecostal World Fellowship. All of these initiatives and responsibilities, synergized with other opportunities during the last two decades, have given me a front-row seat to witness God's mercy and grace flooding the Earth so that the "knowledge of the glory of the Lord" is beginning to cover the Earth as the waters cover the sea.

Empowered21 is a relational network that God birthed in 2010 to help shape the future of the Spirit-empowered movement. It has given leaders around the world a platform to unite and flow together as we focus on the empowerment of the Holy Spirit in the 21st century, new generations, greater unity, and world evangelization. Presently, Empowered21 has fourteen regional cabinets and several auxiliary networks, including a Next-Gen Network, Scholar's Consultation, Discipleship Commission, Global Evangelist Alliance, Global Prayer Alliance, and Global Worship Alliance. Significant, Spirit-empowered leaders from numerous denominations, networks, and every continent form the Empowered21 Global Council, which gives inspirational oversight to this dynamic movement.

In January 2013, while the Empowered21 Global Council was meeting in Honolulu, Hawaii, the network's vision came into focus. The questions among council members at that meeting were simple. "What is something we can do that is so big, no single denomination or network of ministries can do it by themselves?" "What will keep us at the table together for the long term?"

As we prayed about this, several people in the group shared Habakkuk 2:14. The words God had spoken to me years before in my early morning encounter about a new spiritual flood were also shared. The Global Council's energy escalated as we discussed seeing the knowledge of God's glory cover the Earth until every person had an opportunity to encounter Jesus Christ. After several hours of discussion and editing, we adopted the Empowered21 (E21) vision as a commitment by all groups of the council. It is still the driving force holding the E21 network together and drawing us to kingdom collaboration. Our vision is . . .

That every person on Earth would
have an authentic encounter with
Jesus Christ
through the power and presence of
the Holy Spirit . . . by Pentecost 2033.

We chose Pentecost 2033 as our target date because it marks the 2,000-year anniversary of the outpouring of the Holy Spirit, as recorded in Acts Chapter 2, and because it gave us the greatest opportunity to fulfill the vision. Some discussion ensued as to whether the 2,000th anniversary of Jesus' death, burial, resurrection, the giving of the Great Commission, ascension, and the birth of the church at Pentecost was 2033 or 2030, or an even earlier date. Pragmatically, the group chose 2033, which was the date farthest away, to give us as much time as possible to pursue the goal.

This core vision for E21 does not mean that the Global Council believes every person on Earth will accept Jesus as their Savior and Lord (although that would be awesome). What it does mean is that we believe every person on our planet should have an authentic opportunity to intimately know Christ and develop a personal and eternal relationship with the one true God. This is only possible through the power and presence of the Holy Spirit as we once again prioritize the Great Commission in our generation.

To contemplate reaching every person on Earth is certainly an overwhelming vision, but usually, visions from God are beyond our human capabilities.

THINKING TOO
SMALL—MANILA, PHILIPPINES

Just a few months after our meeting in Honolulu, Hawaii, where the Global Council adopted this big vision for Empowered21, I was in Manila, Philippines. In addition to preaching at a church for some friends, I was mobilizing for an upcoming Empowered21 gathering with leaders across the nations in Asia. While in Manila, my travel companion, Assif Reid, and I were invited to a Planetshakers Worship Night at a local Church of God. Since we had the evening off, we decided to attend.

The church was on the outskirts of Manila, and the journey to the concert was more arduous than expected. Manila traffic is legendary, and on that night, Filipino drivers lived up to their billing. When we arrived at the church, the meeting was in full swing. Music thundered from the stage and the auditorium was packed to the brim with young people worshiping Jesus. It was loud, it was exciting, and it was very young. When Assif and I walked in, we spotted a row of older adults (at least older than teenagers) and quickly made our way to join them. The area looked like a safe place for an older guy. At this point in the trip, I was dressed rather casually in jeans and a bright red shirt. This was my first time attending a Planetshakers event, and I had never met any of the Planetshakers team before that night.

Filipino teenagers were screaming, yelling, singing, worshiping, and having a blast. The concert was anointed and powerful. Suddenly, one of the leaders of the group (I would learn later that he was Neil Smith, who served as an executive leader with Planetshakers) took the microphone and stopped the concert. From the stage, he said, "I'm sorry, but I must do this. God just gave me a word." At that, to my surprise, Neil pointed to me and said, "Sir, you, there in the red shirt."

Now, this is something I have been known to do—flowing in the Spirit and giving people words of knowledge—but it is rarely something others do to me. Yet, at that moment, Neil, whom I had never met or seen before, called me out and said, "I've never met you. I don't know who you are or where you are from, but God just told me to speak to you for a minute." His first statement was simply, "God is saying you're thinking too small."

At this statement, I was completely stunned. The E21 Global Council meeting in which we committed to reaching every person on Earth with the gospel by 2033 was only a couple of months in the past. Now, this man was saying I was thinking too small. I didn't know what to do or think!

As I stood there, Neil continued and said, "God's telling me to share with you that Reinhard Bonnke had 100,000 people saved at one time during a crusade, and afterward, he went to his hotel room, and said, 'God, that's it, I can die now. I've had 100,000 people saved in one service.' And the Lord said to him, 'No, you're going to have a million saved in one crusade service someday,' and it happened later on. He was thinking too small."[1]

Neil then told me again, "You're thinking too small." He continued talking about the Great Commission and the people I would reach. This man didn't know me, what I did, where I was from, or that I was even a minister! I was shocked, but I knew in my spirit this was confirmation that we were on track. This E21 vision was on the heart of God, and it was time to think big.

THINKING TOO BROAD—BEAVER CREEK, COLORADO

About a year ago, I was alone praying in a cabin in the mountains as I do each summer, and I began thinking about the E21 vision of reaching every person on Earth. During my prayer time, I asked the Lord, "How can this possibly ever happen? How is everyone in the world going to have a chance to know Jesus?"

In Mark's version of the Great Commission, Jesus says to preach the good news to every single creature, to everyone, every person on Earth. When Jesus gave this command, approximately 300 million people inhabited our planet. Now, the global population is more than eight billion. I was overwhelmed by the magnitude of this task and asked myself and God, "How are we possibly going to reach every person on this planet and help give them a legitimate opportunity to encounter Jesus?" As I asked this question, the Holy Spirit spoke to me clearly. His response was a simple yet profound one. He said this will happen **"One person at a time."**

CHAPTER 1

THE POWER
OF ONE

The smell of gunpowder and scorched earth wafted through the air across the plateau aptly nicknamed, "Hacksaw Ridge." The World War II Battle of Okinawa had raged on this plateau for over a month, and wounded men lay dying across several miles of terrain. This was a grim setting for one of the most powerful examples in history of how God's directive to reach individuals should propel us to action.

"Fall back! Fall back!"

At the frontline of the battle, commanding officers ordered a full-scale retreat as enemy forces launched a major counterattack on their position on May 5, 1945.

"Full retreat! Get to the cliff!"

Soldiers began running for their lives back toward the edge of the ridge, where cargo nets served as makeshift ladders that descended to a stronghold 500 feet below.

Missiles rained down from far-off battleships, and soldiers scrambled over each other in a frantic fury to survive. Amid the chaos, one young medic named Desmond Doss stood still.[2]

As a conscientious objector who refused to kill or carry a weapon, Doss had voluntarily enlisted in the war effort with one singular mission: to save lives. But now, watching his infantry company scramble down the cargo nets while leaving countless casualties behind, his purpose seemed muddled. He had already spent days on end pulling wounded soldiers to this very cliff for medical evacuation. Still, as bullets screamed through the air on all sides and his company retreated, there seemed to be only one reasonable thing to do. He should abandon the combat zone and follow his company to safety.

But at that moment, he felt something stop him— the Spirit of God was moving his heart to consider the impossible.

I can only imagine that this is the moment when common sense must have kicked in. "Come on, Desmond, be realistic. There are thousands of wounded men out there, and you're just one man. You don't even have a gun. You'll be dead in minutes, and you know it. What can you possibly do?"

Nevertheless, at the crossroads of survival and purpose, Desmond made up his mind. He knew exactly what God sent him across the Pacific to do. As he looked back into the clouds of smoke carrying the cries of dying men, he prayed these words:

"Lord, help me get one more."[3]

Those six words embody the burden of God's heart for individuals. They echo the heart cry of the first apostles as they carried the gospel to Asia, Africa, Europe, and the Middle East. They carry forward the call of Moravian missionaries, who abandoned their homes and ventured where none had gone before. They proclaim the cry of the martyrs who, throughout history, have risked everything to reach the unreached and paid the ultimate price along the way.

May each of us feel the power of those words: "Lord, help me get one more."

With his jaw set, Doss charged back into the fray.

Through dust and ashes, Doss evaded enemy soldiers and searched the blistered battlefield for signs of life. Finally, he crawled over a berm and discovered a soldier still breathing—barely. Another medic may have thought it a waste of time to try to help him, but Doss had risked everything to find this one man, and he was not leaving him behind.

With a few assuring words, Doss gave the soldier a shot of morphine before cranking a tourniquet around what remained of his leg. Carrying the soldier over his shoulders, he returned to the cliff's edge, tied a rope around the wounded warrior, angled it around a post to act as a pulley, and lowered the soldier by sheer strength to the bottom.

But Doss was just getting started as he prayed again, "Lord, help me get one more."

And then again.

And again.

And again.

And again.

As the rope burns gradually swelled to blisters on Doss' hands and then began to tear open wider after each new soldier he saved, he continued to pray each time, "Just one more."

One more. I'll risk it all for one more. Even if I die, Lord, help me get one more.

One more.

I'll risk it all for one more.

Even if I die, Lord, help me get one more.

One turned to five, five to ten, ten to twenty, and twenty to forty, and he was just getting started.

"I've got you," Desmond Doss whispered as he slid to the ground beside a soldier and grabbed his arm. Two bullet wounds leaked blood from the soldier's hip and abdomen.

The injured man looked shocked, then managed a shallow grin.

"Desmond. I never thought I'd be this glad to see you."

Desmond bandaged the wounds as best he could and then looked the soldier in the eyes.

"You're going to make it. Let's get you out of here; how's that sound?"

The soldier nodded, and Desmond lifted him onto his shoulders.

At another point, while searching the underground cave system beneath the battlefield, Doss even came face to face with a wounded enemy soldier in desperate need of medical attention. At that moment, Doss knew God's heart toward this man was no different than for any of the others—ally or enemy, in good health or seemingly hopeless. God's heart was the same—one more . . . just one more.

As the wounded soldier tried frantically to stand and run, Doss raised his hands to show he was unarmed. Then, ever so slowly, he pulled a morphine shot and bandages from his pack. When the soldier finally settled down with a bewildered look, Doss began to tend his wounds.

The number of people Desmond Doss saved in those initial twelve hours is estimated anywhere from seventy-five to more than one hundred, but when he ran back onto that battlefield, he had no idea how many lives he would save in the end. He just knew that one more would be worth it all.

Not a million. Not ten thousand. Not a hundred. One. Just one.

Each one mattered. They not only mattered to Doss, but he knew that each person mattered to God. God's heart is for each individual on Earth. For every single one.

Several days later, amid an allied maneuver, a grenade went off at Doss' feet sending shattered shrapnel up his leg to his hip. He tended his wound as best he could before attempting to crawl to safety. In doing so, he was shot in the arm by a sniper. But even then, as litter-bearers came to his aid, he insisted they take the wounded man beside him first.[4]

One more.

C.S. Lewis once wrote, "[Jesus] died not for men but for each man. If each man had been the only man made, He would have done no less."[5] Every person created has inherent value, worth, and importance to God. The motivation for the cross was to provide a way of rescue for every single person ever to walk the Earth. May we see people the way God does—not just in masses, but as individuals in need of God's saving grace. The adage is true: "If you were the only person on Earth, Jesus still would have died for you."

Like Doss, the challenge before us may look impossible. I imagine his hesitancy when he first began going after those wounded and dying soldiers. Similarly, we may ask, "How do we reach a population of more than eight billion people that continues growing every day?" Rather than being overwhelmed by the task, may we be so full of the Holy Spirit that in our hearts, we hear and echo the cry of Desmond Doss, "Lord, help me get one more!"

EIGHT BILLION!

On November 15, 2022, the United Nations reported that the world population reached eight billion people and is expected to reach eight and one-half billion by 2030.[6] Moreover, the number continues to climb by sixty-seven million people per year.[7]

Most of us have never contemplated what eight billion really means. Maybe these facts will put this mega-number in perspective:

If you were eight billion seconds old, you would be 254 years old.

If every person on Earth held hands in a line, they would wrap around the Earth 335 times.

Stack eight billion pennies together and you'd make a tower 6,960 miles high.

Just to count to eight billion would take a lifetime, possibly 100 years or more, depending on how fast you were to count.

Since approximately only thirty percent of these eight billion people presently identify themselves as followers of Christ,[8] our task remains monumental. How will we ever reach so many people and give every single one a legitimate opportunity to have an encounter with Jesus Christ? The answer remains: one person at a time.

> **By reaching one, God will help us reach the masses.**

By reaching one, God will help us reach the masses. Everyone must be reached. Everyone can be reached.

EveryONE.

ONE IS POWERFUL

There are numerous examples throughout history of how one vote, one person, and one decision changed history. One, the smallest cardinal number of seemingly little significance, has the power to bring about tremendous change—both positive and negative.

In 1800, Thomas Jefferson was elected President of the United States by one vote cast by Alexander Hamilton in the House of Representatives after a tie in the electoral college.[9]

In 1875, one vote changed France from a monarchy to a republic.[10]

In the 1400s, one man, by the name of Johannes Gutenberg, through the enhancement of printing technology, brought the Word of God to the common person.[11]

In 1933, one man, Adolf Hitler, came to power in Germany, and his reign sparked World War II, which brought destruction across the globe and the Holocaust, during which over six million European Jews were killed.[12]

In 1955, one brave lady named Rosa Parks refused to give up her seat on a Montgomery, Alabama, bus. This one courageous act ignited a civil rights movement that forever changed the landscape of racial equality.[13]

In 1973, one misguided woman named Norma McCorvey filed a suit against the state of Texas. Her case eventually reached the Supreme Court, resulting in the decision known as Roe v. Wade,[14] which legalized the abortion of more than 63 million babies in the United

States.[15] It was not until 2022 that the Supreme Court overturned Roe v. Wade.[16]

In 1983, one Russian soldier named Stanislav Petrov chose not to report a potential nuclear strike to Soviet Union leaders. Dismissing the computer's detection as a false alarm, his one decision prevented retaliation and saved the world from nuclear disaster.[17]

The list could go on and on. One vote, one person, or one decision has the power to affect change and impact millions of people for generations to come—for better or for worse. The smallest natural number, one is powerful.

BESSIE, MAUDE, AND LISA

My grandmother Bessie (Amos) Wilson was a preacher and a very good one. She won hundreds of people to Christ in her early ministry and preached numerous successful revival campaigns. She was such an effective preacher that one night during an altar call, a rough young man left the back pew and gave his heart to Christ. That young man was M. E. Wilson, my grandfather. A short time after his conversion, he married Bessie Amos, joining her in ministry. For the single young ladies reading this book: Bessie's method was very effective! If you don't have a husband, preach one out!

During those early years of her evangelistic ministry, Bessie went to a small town in the hills of Virginia for a two-week revival. Usually, a revival with Bessie Wilson as an evangelist was a powerful week of ministry with dozens of lives touched and multiple people being converted. This two-week revival in Virginia was a significant exception.

Night after night, she would preach her heart out, and no one responded. The meetings were dead, and spiritual plowing was tough. Nothing was moving. Night after night, the dearth continued.

"Is there anyone here tonight who would like to accept Jesus as their Savior and give their life to Him?"

Silence filled the room.

"Anyone?"

Nothing.

And then one night, a single little girl timidly stood up. Her eyes glistened with new hope as my grandmother made eye contact with her and smiled. This young girl was the only convert for the entire two weeks. My grandmother left Virginia, believing that the revival was a significant failure.

Years later, as my grandmother and grandfather continued in their ministry and touched countless more lives, a young lady approached Bessie during a large convention. She was wearing a nice suit and held a Bible under her arm.

"Excuse me, Sister Wilson, do you remember me?"

My grandmother studied the young woman and searched her memory but could not recall having met her.

"Honey, I'm so sorry, I don't! Have we met before?"

The young woman smiled, and said, "Do you remember preaching a revival in the mountains of Virginia in a little town years ago?"

My grandmother thought about it and then nodded.

"I sure do, honey. And you know what? I think that was the worst revival I've ever preached in my life! If I remember right, I preached for two whole weeks. In the end, we only had one conversion, a little child."

At that moment, the corners of the young woman's eyes filled with tears.

"Please don't say that, Sister Wilson. You have no idea what that revival meant to that one little girl. The child who gave her life to Jesus was me."

The young lady's name was Maude, and she had become a preacher in the many years since that revival in her small hometown. Maude married a man named Martin, so she became known as Maude Martin. She and her husband served as state leaders in their denomination and were recognized for their effective ministry. Bessie had no idea what that one little girl, who found Jesus during those two hard weeks of ministry, would do for God. We never fully see the potential in one life.

Now, fast forward sixty years from those tough two weeks in the Virginia mountains and flip scenes to Kentucky, where I had just married my beautiful wife, Lisa. She was instrumental in leading me to Jesus. When I gave my life to Him and was filled with the Holy Spirit, I began to bring Lisa around Spirit-filled, Spirit-empowered services. Yet, Lisa still had not experienced the baptism of the Holy Spirit.

For the first year of our marriage, Lisa sought the Holy Spirit at almost every service she attended. She was always in the front, praying and asking God to fill her. Every time an altar call was given, Lisa went forward. She was hungry for more of God.

Lisa marched around the church. She laid on her face. She screamed out loud. She sat in silence. She did and tried everything the Pentecostal people around her told her to do, but she still had not received Spirit baptism.

During that season, our pastor in Owensboro, Kentucky, announced that the church was going to have a revival. Lisa and I committed to attending every service. The evangelists ministering in the revival were an elderly couple, probably in their seventies. They took turns preaching each night. Honestly, the husband was not the most exciting preacher

I had ever heard—far from it. Yet, when his wife preached, everything seemed to shift. She was anointed, engaging, and had a special touch that ignited your hunger for more of the Lord. Although she was over the age of seventy, this evangelist was a fireball of passion and spiritual zeal.

Every other night, when she preached and extended the invitation to receive the Holy Spirit, Lisa went forward. And then one night, this elderly minister connected with Lisa and helped her to experience the fullness of the Holy Spirit. Gently and gracefully, the evangelist helped her receive God's power into her life in a fresh way. It was wonderful.

That moment of spiritual experience was invaluable in Lisa's journey, empowering her life and mission for the Lord. We simply could not have done or continued doing all the assignments God has blessed us to accomplish without Lisa being full of the Holy Spirit. Her powerful prayers and supernatural insight have pulled us through over and over again. I am privileged to have Lisa as my wife and grateful God filled her with His Spirit during that revival.

Perhaps, the most amazing part of the story is that when we put the pieces together, we realized that this elderly evangelist was saved many years earlier in a small-town revival in Virginia when she was just a little girl. The revival was held by Bessie (Amos) Wilson. The person who led my wife into a greater spiritual experience was Maude Martin, the little girl who had been saved in my grandmother's revival so many years before. God used her to impact my wife a generation later.

One preacher—my grandmother—preaching at one revival in which one little girl was saved has resulted in my wife receiving the baptism of the Holy Spirit and thousands of people being blessed through Maude's ministry many years later. Never underestimate the power of one!

EVERY PERSON IS SOME MOTHER'S CHILD

Thirty years ago, just as communism collapsed in Ukraine and Westerners were being allowed into the country for the first time, I was invited to come and preach. We flew into Moscow and embarked on a journey for an entire day and night, driving through some of the coldest weather I've ever experienced. The Russian cold had been etched in my memory since we were in a car with almost no heat. Numerous questions filled my thoughts before the trip, and now in one of the coldest rides of my life through the Russian winter, I found myself second-guessing if the trip was going to be worth it.

Though the Iron Curtain was falling, many Russians and Ukrainians remained hostile toward Western foreigners and Christians. Our team was briefed on various safety concerns, and I had been cautioned by several people in authority against going on the trip. For several months before saying yes, my mind and heart wrestled back and forth regarding the decision to go. One week, I was excited, and the next week, the trip just seemed too difficult and risky. Yet, here I was, bouncing along on treacherous roads, wondering if I would freeze to death on our first full day in the former USSR.

Could this trip possibly be worth the risks, the expense, and the pain?

As I rode on the pothole-infested Russian roads in the middle of the night with an inch of ice on the inside of an extremely old car, I wasn't sure. Yet, in praying about the trip, I had decided it would be better to try than miss the opportunity since the eternal destiny of someone might be at stake. When Jesus gave the Great Commission, He didn't say for us to evaluate the risks, and if we found the risks were low, we could go preach the gospel. Quite the opposite, He commanded us to go, whatever the risks, noting that many would become martyrs in the process.

Ultimately, we arrived in Eastern Ukraine at a city called Sloviansk, which would be our home base, and began traveling around the region holding evangelistic meetings. From public auditoriums to public squares and from schools to churches, we moved from city to city across Eastern Ukraine, sharing the gospel anywhere and everywhere we possibly could. The host worship team led worship, I preached, and the Holy Spirit worked in ways I had never seen before. We seemed to be experiencing a bit of heaven on Earth. I would invite the people to respond to the gospel, "If you want to give your life to Jesus today, stand up!" and the entire attendance of 1,500 people in a city auditorium would stand, or an entire class of high school students would pray to receive Jesus as Savior.

During this amazing season, the spiritual vacuum created by communism was inhaling the good news of Jesus in mighty gulps, and we were privileged to witness it. The spiritual hunger behind the Iron Curtain was palpable and unlike anything our team had ever seen. I had never been in a riper harvest field, which was filled with desperation. For the evangelist in me, this was a dream come true.

I could tell more of this story, but please allow me the opportunity to share an important lesson God taught me on that first and subsequent ministry trips to Ukraine: *Always err on the side of attempting to obey the Great Commission.* When you wonder, "Should I share the gospel with them or not?" "Should I spend the extra money for that outreach?" "Should I make the extra effort to reach out and serve them?" "Should I go to these people or not?"— here's your answer: Go! Go as far as you can, as fast you can, while you can. Jesus has already given the command for us to go. We do not need to wait for a directive. He is with you, and unless He stops you, He wants you to go and share His good news with one and all at every opportunity He provides.

On a subsequent visit to Ukraine, we found ourselves ministering in the city of Kharkiv (Kharkov at the time) in Freedom Square, the central square of the city. (Freedom Square is where one of the early missile strikes occurred and the Russian-Ukrainian war began. The missile exploded in the square, doing significant damage to this beautiful public gathering place where years before, the gospel of Jesus exploded as we held a large crusade.) Hundreds of people were saved and healed during our special afternoon meeting in Kharkiv. We experienced a mighty anointing there, and hundreds of people came to Jesus—which was awesome. Yet, one of the most important moments of the day happened outside the view of people on the square.

We completed the ministry time for the night, and people were leaving to go home. As I opened the door to enter my awaiting car, a huge, burly man who looked like he was on the Ukrainian weightlifting team grabbed me by the shirt and yanked me toward him like a rag doll. He pulled me close to his face with both hands. His eyes were red, and his breath smelled profusely of Vodka. I was startled by this giant of a man, and if I had taken time to contemplate my situation, I would have been afraid.

Through clenched teeth and a deep voice that sounded sort of like a grizzly bear, the man spoke in English saying, "I hate Americans!"

Unsure if I would live, I stared back at the man glaring down at me. Yet, at that moment, God moved me to speak before I even had a chance to think about what I was going to say. I heard myself proclaim: "You may hate me, but I love you, and God loves you."

My words hung in the air for what felt like minutes until unexpectedly, this burly, weightlifter-sized man broke. Tears filled his eyes, his grip on my shirt went limp, and his body fell forward against me. There, in a darkened parking lot, I held him as he wept on my shoulder. After a minute, the man was able to compose and sober himself enough to tell me his name along with a little bit of his story. Right then and there, at the door of my car, he gave his life to Jesus.

What we later learned was that his mother, who lived in Kharkiv, was a believer. She had been praying and regularly fasting for her son for years. The entire community of believers rejoiced with her when they heard of his miraculous conversion.

My encounter with this man in Ukraine serves as a reminder that each person we encounter is someone's son or daughter, brother or sister, mom or dad. I ask myself often, "Wouldn't you want someone to reach out to your lost loved one and draw them to Jesus? Wouldn't you want someone to go out of their way, pay the extra expense, ride through the frozen tundra, or endure imminent danger to reach your child if it meant the difference between heaven and hell?"

In a brief moment one night, God allowed me to participate in His answer to a mother's prayer for her lost son, who finally embraced a relationship with Jesus Christ. Whatever the cost or sacrifice, "Please, Lord give us one more."

CHAPTER 2

A RESTLESS SHEPHERD

First-century shepherding was a unique profession requiring significant attentiveness and skill. Faithfully, day in and day out, the shepherd was expected to care for his sheep with focused vigilance and tender care. He cleaned their stables or caves, fed them, sheared their wool, called them by unique names, and counted them one by one. Let's explore the account of one good shepherd.

The night was falling, and the sheep were calming for the evening. It had been a seemingly fine day for the flock. As the shepherd surveyed them one last time before resting his own weary body, his count kept falling short by one. His math skills must be slipping, he thought. Yet, with every single count, his total was ninety-nine instead of the one hundred that were part of the fold. As he looked more closely, he noted that indeed one of the sheep was missing.

He quickly began to call the sheep by name hoping that this wayward one was behind a nearby bush or simply being overlooked. Yet, he heard no response. Ninety-nine of his sheep were accounted for, but one was missing. His heart sank, and without a second thought, he decided to go sheep searching. The shepherd made certain the ninety-nine sheep were secure before he grabbed his oil lamp, instructed his sheepdog to stay with the flock, and headed into the night searching for the missing one.

Hours passed, darkness gave way to sunshine, and still, there was no sign of the lost sheep. Most shepherds would have given up after one night of searching. After all, periodically losing a few sheep was to be expected. A shepherd in 1st-century Judea would have been prepared to lose at least five percent of his flock each year. To live through a year or even certain seasons of the year and only lose *one* sheep were pretty good odds. A ninety-nine percent rating would be considered an A+ on anyone's grading scale. Most would judge that as an exceptional job. But not this shepherd! The thought of abandoning his search or settling for the loss of one never even crossed his mind.

The shepherd pushed through his weariness and sleepiness. His legs burned, and his stomach churned. He could not bear the thought of a single one of his sheep being injured or destroyed while away from the flock. Whatever was required, he must find it.

Finally, he saw the wayward sheep on the horizon, laying still and looking afraid. The sheep's hoof was caught in a crevice in the rocks. The bleating had given way to resignation as the sheep surrendered to the trap and was now waiting for certain destruction by predators or from starvation. He was off the beaten path, and yes, the sheep was reaping the consequences of his wayward ways.

The trapped sheep's only hope was for the shepherd to find him.

Quickly, the shepherd ran to his sheep, and without chastening it or berating it for its rebellion, he released it from the trap. He took the sheep in his arms, placed it on his shoulders, and carried it toward the fold where the other sheep were secured. Along the way, he called out to his neighboring shepherds, "Rejoice with me! I have found my lost sheep."

Imagine the scene when Jesus told this parable to a crowd of tax collectors and sinners who had gathered around, longing to hear what the Teacher had to say. Pharisees—highly respected teachers of the Law—were also in the crowd. Jesus' encounters with them often involved a reproof for their staunchly held religious practices and hypocrisy. Earlier, one of the Pharisees had shouted from the crowd, "This man, Jesus, welcomes sinners and eats with them! Can you believe it?" (Luke 15:2, paraphrased) At that moment, Jesus began sharing three parables with the crowd, starting with the Parable of the Lost Sheep.

The beloved Teacher was illustrating that when a sheep has gone astray, any good shepherd willingly leaves the ninety-nine in search of the one. The shepherd will be restless as long as even *one* sheep is missing. He loves the sheep in his fold, but his heart is passionately concerned with the one that is lost. Millions of people are like lost sheep, trapped by their waywardness, facing certain destruction, and desperately needing to be found.

Peter gives us a further glimpse into God's heart when he insists: "[The Lord] is patient with you, not wanting anyone to perish, but everyone to come to repentance" (2 Peter 3:9). God wants everyone, and He is calling us to join Him—the persistent shepherd—and help bring them home.

LOST IN THE HOUSE

Following the Parable of the Lost Sheep, Jesus continued: "Or suppose a woman has ten silver coins and loses one.

Doesn't she light a lamp, sweep the house, and search carefully until she finds it?" (Luke 15:8).

This parable is different from the first because the coin is lost in the house. In the first parable, the sheep wanders far away, so the shepherd goes to find him. In this second parable, a woman was looking for a coin she had lost inside her home. She swept the house and searched diligently until she found it, and when she finally did, she called to her friends and neighbors, "Rejoice with me; I have found my lost coin" (Luke 15:9).

This parable reminds us that you don't have to be in a faraway place to be lost. You may attend church every week, be engaged in ministry, be right in the house, and yet still be lost. God is searching; He is sweeping, and He is fully engaged in finding every single one, far and near.

> **God is searching; He is sweeping, and He is fully engaged in finding every single one, far and near.**

When this woman found the coin, she rejoiced and invited others to rejoice with her. On both occasions, in the Parable of the Lost Sheep and the Parable of the Lost Coin, Jesus emphasized that when something or someone is lost and then found, it is time for rejoicing. The Pharisees should have been delighted with what was happening! Instead, they were bothered by a Rabbi who would engage with sinners and tax collectors.

THE PARABLE OF THE LOST SON

Jesus concluded His parabolic trilogy with one of the best-known stories in Scripture.

The story began: "There was a man who had two sons. The younger one said to his father, 'Father, give me my share of the estate'" (Luke 15:11-12).

In ancient Jewish culture, a father's wealth would have been divided among his sons at his passing. A son asking for his portion of the inheritance before the father's passing would have been considered extremely disrespectful. However, the father resolved to grant his son's request anyway.

With his newfound wealth, the son turned his back on his father and family and headed out on his own to live an extravagant life. He spent his entire inheritance on frivolous and wild living.

As the weeks turned to months and the months turned to years, the father lived with a constant eye on the horizon, his heart aching for his son, longing to see him back where he belonged—at home.

Jesus continued the parable, saying, "After he had spent everything, there was a severe famine in that whole country, and he began to be in need. So, he went and hired himself out to a citizen of that country, who sent him to his fields to feed pigs. He longed to fill his stomach with the pods that the pigs were eating, but no one gave him anything" (vv. 15–16).

Of all the work a young Jewish man could have, feeding pigs would have been at the bottom of the food chain. Jews were not allowed to eat pigs since they were considered unclean animals under Mosaic law. They would not even mention their name. To feed pigs was filthy, nasty work. If you've ever been to a pig pen, you know it is a dirty place. This was a physically horrible place, and even more so, the pig pen was a spiritual nightmare. The wayward son was at rock bottom, living like an animal. While feeding the pigs, he became hungry and was even tempted to share in some of the pigs' slop—YUCK!

This young man was far away from home, hungry, depleted, and debased without legal standing in a foreign country. He was broke and broken, humiliated by his failure.

Jesus continued the story: "When he came to his senses, he said, 'How many of my father's hired servants have food to spare, and here I am starving to death! I will set out and go back to my father and say to him: Father, I have sinned against heaven and against you. I am no longer worthy to be called your son; make me like one of your hired servants'" (vv. 17–19).

The son stumbled toward home. With his clothes torn, his pockets empty, his ego smashed, and the stench of pig manure emanating from him, the formerly wealthy Jewish boy had now hit bottom, and the world could see his ruin. Yet, despite his lost son's changed countenance and broken spirit, the father easily recognized him, and his heart overflowed with love.

"But while he was still a long way off, his father saw him and was filled with compassion for him; he ran to his son, threw his arms around him and kissed him" (v. 20).

The joy that overwhelmed this father at seeing his lost son return home was inexplicable!

"The son said to him, 'Father, I have sinned against heaven and against you. I am no longer worthy to be called your son'" (v. 21).

But the father didn't even take notice of his son's words, yelling instead to his servants, "Quick! Bring the best robe and put it on him. Put a ring on his finger and sandals on his feet. Bring the fattened calf and kill it. Let's have a feast and celebrate. For this son of mine was dead and is alive again; he was lost and is found" (vv. 22–24).

The lost sheep, the lost coin, and the lost son.

Jesus couldn't remain silent at the religious leader's disposition toward the ones who needed the gospel the most, and he used these three different lessons to portray God's heart. When the sheep wandered off, the shepherd went and found him. When the coin was lost in the house, the woman remained and searched the house diligently. Finally, when the son left his father and squandered his inheritance, the father waited with anticipation for his return. In each narrative, people rejoice when the lost is found!

God's heart is continually moved for the lost. How about your heart?

A HEART FOR THE LOST

In God's kingdom today, we stand on the shoulders of spiritual giants who were committed to reaching the lost. They lived with a "whatever it takes" attitude, and no sacrifice was too great.

David Brainerd was an early missionary to the Delaware Indians on the continent of North America.[18]

Several years ago, I attended a meeting held in Northampton, Massachusetts, where he is buried. I was able to find Brainerd's gravestone in a historic cemetery in Northampton. This passionate missionary said, "I care not where I live, or what hardships I go through so that I can but gain souls to Christ. While I am asleep, I dream of these things; as soon as I awake, the first thing I think of is this great work. All my desire is the conversion of sinners, and all my hope is in God."[19] Brainerd married Jonathan Edward's daughter and died of tuberculosis at the young age of twenty-nine. He sacrificed all to pursue the lost.

Dr. John Geddie carried his passion for reaching one wherever he went.[20] A humble Presbyterian missionary, he journeyed to the shores of Vanuatu, an island in the South Pacific. For twenty-four years, he preached the gospel, tirelessly working to bring the message of salvation to the people. The legacy of his ministry is engraved on a tablet in his church: "When he landed in 1848, there were no Christians. When he left, in 1872, there were no heathen."[21]

William Booth, the great founder of the Salvation Army,[22] was invited by King Edward VII to Buckingham Palace in 1904. It was a big day for Booth, who had labored in the squalors of London and throughout England, helping the broken and hurting. He established an army of people for the gospel, and his work was noticed by royalty, who invited him to the palace. When the king asked Booth, who was 75 years old, to sign the autograph book that every guest signed, Booth wrote: *"Your Majesty, Some men's passion is for gold, some men's passion is for art, some men's passion is for fame. My passion is for souls."*[23]

> **"Your Majesty, Some men's passion is for gold, some men's passion is for art, some men's passion is for fame. My passion is for souls."**
> **–William Booth**

THE AUCA INDIANS OF ECUADOR

One of the greatest missionary stories of all time is about a group of young missionaries and their devotion to an isolated tribe in the depths of the Amazon rainforest. Books, such as *Through Gates of Splendor* by Elisabeth Elliot, and movies, like *End of the Spear*, recount events in the Ecuadorian jungle in the 1950s.[24]

Isolated from the world was the Waorani tribe, also known as "Auca," meaning savage, a term given by neighboring tribes. The name seemed fitting for this group of people that wielded spears against all outsiders and were the most violent tribe known in the area, having killed numerous members of other tribes and oil company workers near their territory. But for five young missionaries, the knowledge of this tribe's violent ways and self-imposed isolation didn't cause them to run but stirred their hearts.

In 1956, Jim Elliot, Nate Saint, Ed McCully, Pete Fleming, and Roger Youderian united at a missionary outpost in Arajuno, Ecuador, engaging with the local Quichua indigenous group at the forefront of the global missionary effort. At this outpost, everyone knew of the notorious Waoranis deeper in the jungle to the east. Still, for centuries, their only recorded interaction with outsiders was with the rubber hunters who swept through the jungle in the early 1900s burning villages and enslaving the people to work as laborers extracting latex from the trees. This interaction only intensified the Waorani's distrust and disdain toward outsiders.

Yet, for these young missionaries, this raised one critical question: "If we don't share the gospel with them, who will?" They seemed to be echoing the apostle Paul's words to the Romans: "How, then, can they call on the one they have not believed in? And how can they believe in the one of whom they have not heard? And how can they hear without someone preaching to them?" (Romans 10:14).

After months of praying and planning, Nate Saint, the group's pilot, touched his yellow Piper PA-14 plane down on a long sandbar along the Curaray River, only a few miles from the Waorani village, they established a campsite. At the same time, Nate Saint returned to the skies to fly over the Waorani village and get their attention.

Leading up to this, the missionaries had strategically flooded the Waorani people with gifts using a pulley system on the plane, and they had recruited the help of a Waorani refugee named Dayuma, who taught them a collection of friendly Waorani phrases that they shouted down at the people with a public-address speaker system attached to the plane.

For several days, Nate continued to fly over the Waorani village using the speakers to shout their friendly phrases, such as "Biti miti punimupa," which meant, "I like you; I want to be your friend," and "Biti winki pungi amupa," meaning, "I want to approach you," or, more colloquially, "Let's get together." Finally, he included a new directive: "Come to the Curaray Apa (River)."

On January 6, 1956, the five missionaries were walking about their campsite, all relentlessly shouting Auca phrases into the jungle. And then, as Ed finished one of his phrases, the hearts of the missionaries jumped as a clear masculine voice boomed out, answering their call.

From the dense foliage, three Aucas emerged, stepping onto the sandy shore across the river from the missionaries' campsite. They were a young man and two women; all clothed only in strings tied around their waists, wrists, and thighs. The missionaries, momentarily struck speechless by their unexpected appearance, finally managed to exclaim in unison, "Puinani! (welcome!)"

Over the next several hours, they spoke as well as they could with the people and shared food and gifts with them. They took a young man, whom they called George, on a flight over the village, during which he had the time of his life shouting to his shocked friends down below. It appeared that the missionaries had made a great first connection and were on their way to reaching the Waorani. However, two days later, on January 8, everything changed.

Unknown to the missionaries, intertribal drama had stirred among the Waorani tribesmen. To save his reputation, George fabricated a story about how the missionaries had attacked them. Determined to retaliate, the leader of the group—a warrior named Mincaye—called for a counterattack.

On January 8, Mincaye and a group of spear-wielding warriors attacked and killed the five missionaries who had come to share the gospel with them. These men had risked their lives to reach the Waorani people, and they paid the ultimate price.

Following these events, Dayuma, the Waorani refugee who had helped the missionaries assemble phrases from her native language, became closely connected with the missionaries' wives and was moved deeply in the aftermath of the missionaries' death. Broken-hearted that her people had killed the husbands of women with whom she'd developed friendships, she became determined to return to the tribe and tell them they could safely interact with these people, and that they had no need for killing anymore.

Several years later, Dayuma came with several members of her tribe to invite Elisabeth Elliot (the wife of missionary Jim Elliot) and Rachel Saint (the sister of missionary Nate Saint) to come and live with them in the village.

Now that's crazy! Who in their right mind would accept an invitation to go and live with the same violent Stone Age tribe that killed your husband and brother? But Elisabeth was as brave as her husband and had been studying the people's language and praying since his death that the Lord would send her to the tribe.

In the years that followed, as Elisabeth and Rachel ministered to the people, the heart of Mincaye was moved by the Holy Spirit. After giving his life to Jesus, he insisted on being baptized right away. Many other Waorani gave their lives to Jesus. Men and women, willing to go where no one else had dared to go before with a passion burning in their hearts for lost souls, brought previously unreached people to the knowledge of Christ.

THE BIBLELESS PEOPLE

Cameron Townsend was born in California in 1896 during a time of poverty.[25] He was raised in the Presbyterian Church, and when the time came for him to attend college, he went to Occidental College in Los Angeles. During his time at Occidental College, he became involved in the Student Volunteer movement. One of its leaders, John R. Mott, visited Occidental College and challenged students to dedicate their lives to spreading the gospel around the world.[26] Townsend, inspired by Mott, joined a Bible association that sold Spanish Bibles, and in 1917, he departed for Guatemala to distribute the Bibles. Once there, he placed God's Word in the hands of many Guatemalans, but he soon realized many of the people could not speak Spanish. The majority of the native people only spoke the Cakchiquel language. One Cakchiquel man Townsend met asked, "If your God is so great, why can't He speak my language?"[27] This challenged Townsend, who began learning the Cakchiquel tongue and, within ten years, translated the New Testament.

As the Cakchiquel people were finally able to engage with God's Word, many were saved. As a result, Townsend rejoiced in winning these lost souls for the Lord, but he was still troubled by the question that earlier had been posed to him. "If your God is so great, why can't He speak my language?" Day and night, this question haunted Townsend as he thought of people worldwide without God's Word in their native tongue. Seeking direction, Townsend decided to share his burden with a group of missionaries in Chicago, who advised him to stay in Guatemala and dedicate his life to the Cakchiquels.

However, their advice did not settle well with him. Townsend was deeply troubled and restless and could not shake free of his burden. In desperation, he cried out to God for clarity and guidance. Immediately, he opened his Bible and laid his finger on a random verse. When he looked down, he read these words: "What do you think? If a man has a hundred sheep, and one goes astray, does he not leave the ninety-nine and go to the mountains to seek the one straying?" (Matthew 18:12). At that moment, Townsend knew what God was calling him to do, and with a surrendered heart he prayed, "Yes, Lord. I'll leave the 250,000 Cakchiquel and go in quest of the Bibleless peoples."[28]

PREPARED FOR EVERYONE

Years ago, I was on my way to New York City to preach at a ministry gathering. I was emerging from the holiday season in which I had indulged in time with family, TV, and a lot of good food! I was on an airplane heading to my first ministry assignment of the new year. I had been upgraded to first class and gratefully accepted this unexpected blessing. I boarded the plane, loaded my bag into the overhead compartment, and grabbed my Bible before sitting down to use the flight time to go over my message.

When I sat down, I noticed a young man sitting in the window seat next to my aisle seat. He was a young, Hispanic man, probably in his late teens, with baggy jeans, a graphic t-shirt, and multiple piercings. When I was seated, the young man looked over and asked, "Is that a Bible?" After I said "yes," he replied, "I need that!"

This should have immediately been my cue to minister to this young man. What an opportunity! I have ministered to fellow passengers on flights before, sometimes even leading them to salvation, and here was a young man stating to me that he needed the Bible. Yet, I wasn't prepared for the moment. Spiritually lethargic following the holiday season, I chose not to engage. Instead, I exchanged a few pleasantries with him before leaning back with my Bible in hand and falling asleep.

As the captain announced our descent into the city, I was suddenly awakened by what felt like someone prodding me. The nudge came from the Holy Spirit, who reminded me of the young man sitting next to me and the opportunity I was missing. I finally began to do what I should have done all along. I engaged with this weary-looking young man and ministered to him.

As I did, I learned his name was Gabriel, and he had grown up as a pastor's kid. He was recently involved with some peers in a Midwestern state doing things that were against the law, and now he was moving to the East Coast to get away from the bad crowd and search for a new beginning. Although he grew up around Christianity, he was unaware of how to become a believer and develop a personal relationship with Jesus.

I shared my testimony with him and continued talking to him until we parted ways at baggage claim. Though aware of his need for God's Word, Gabriel did not receive Christ that day, and I grieved in my heart that I had not taken the opportunity to minister to him sooner. I was not ready for the one God put in my path.

Are we guilty of cultivating comfort when we should be living with the compassionate heart of the shepherd? Are we ready for the opportunities God will give us today to share His love? Are we looking for the one who is lost? We don't have to go to the far shores of the South Pacific or the depths of the Ecuadorian jungle to find them. They are all around us. The broken, bound, and beaten. They need hope and the message we know so well. They need us to remain restless until they are found.

We don't have to go to the far shores of the South Pacific or the depths of the Ecuadorian jungle to find them. They are all around us.

So, refuse to repose, scan the horizon, pursue the wayward, sweep the house, free the trapped, and join God's party as the lost are found.

CHAPTER 3

REACHING THE MULTITUDES BY REACHING ONE

In 1963, meteorologist and mathematician Edward Lorenz coined the term "butterfly effect"[29] by presenting a theory to the New York Academy that stated a butterfly could flap its wings and set molecules of air in motion, which would move other molecules of air in motion and so on, resulting in a hurricane on the other side of the world. Lorenz's proposal was considered ridiculous and was not taken seriously. However, it was an intriguing idea that stuck around in science fiction for years until, in the mid-1990s, the butterfly effect was finally proven true by physics professors worldwide. The butterfly effect is now known as *the law of sensitive dependence upon initial conditions*, and it doesn't apply to just butterflies. The effect impacts any form of matter, including people.

This idea that one molecule in motion could cause a ripple effect that spreads around the world can be used to demonstrate how the smallest action a person makes matters and affects not only their lives but the lives of others near and far, even affecting generations to come. One great example of this began with the Nobel Peace Prize-winning scientist Norman Borlaug.

In 1970, Norman Borlaug was awarded the Nobel Peace Prize for developing a hybridized variety of wheat that could survive drought. His work was recognized for saving more than one billion people around the world from starvation and famine. This was an accomplishment worth recognizing! However, if you examine things closely, you will find much more to this story.

Before Borlaug, there was a man named Henry Wallace who served as vice president of the United States during Franklin D. Roosevelt's third presidential term. Wallace was previously the secretary of agriculture. He used his position as vice president and his previous experience to create an agricultural research station in Mexico, which was used to hybridize corn and wheat for arid climates. Because of his other duties, he could not operate the research station, so he hired a young man named Norman Borlaug for the task. One might say that Wallace, not

Borlaug, should be credited with saving more than a billion lives from starvation and famine. Unless, of course, there was someone before Wallace.

Actually, before Norman Borlaug and Henry Wallace, was a man named George Washington Carver. George Washington Carver is most famous for discovering 266 uses for the peanut and eighty-eight uses for the sweet potato, many of which we still utilize today. At nineteen years old, Carver attended Iowa State University as the only African American student on campus. He developed a close mentoring relationship with his science professor, who allowed his six-year-old son to join Carver's weekend botanical outings. Carver inspired the young boy who developed an interest in agriculture and botany and showed him how plants could help humanity. This six-year-old boy's name was Henry Wallace.

However, the story doesn't end there. Before George Washington Carver, there was a young, white farming couple who lived in Missouri in the mid-19th century, Moses and Susan Carver. They encountered trouble one January night after the Civil War when the Quantrill's Raiders, who were known for bringing destruction to black communities, came to the town where the Carvers lived. They destroyed the Carver's farm, killing multiple people and capturing Mary Washington, the Carver's one slave, and her baby son, George, whom she refused to let go. As a result of these horrific events, Moses went after the Quantrill by horse, traveling several hours north to meet the raiders and rescue young George. He gave his last horse to the men in exchange for the infant's release. Moses then traveled the five-day journey by foot with George back to the farm where he and his wife, Susan, raised the child as their own, knowing his mother was now dead. Considering these events, should Moses and Susan Carver be the ones credited with saving one billion people from starvation?

But wait a moment! The narrative doesn't end there. While Moses and Susan Carver saved and raised a child who would eventually become the man who contributed much to society and affected history-making events, Moses and Susan's parents should be credited with raising them to live good and productive lives. We could go on and on, but I think the point is clear.

You see, while Norman Borlaug won the Nobel Peace Prize for his green revolution, the individuals and their actions before him led to one billion people being saved from starvation and famine.[30]

One life and one action can set in motion more than we realize. This is the butterfly effect. The Apostle Paul reminded the church in Ephesus that our God "is able to do immeasurably more than all we ask or imagine, according to his power that is at work within us . . ." (Ephesians 3:20). We must never underestimate the latent potential in one person.

> **We must never underestimate the latent potential in one person.**

ALL OF THAT FOR ONE MAN?

Jesus preached to multitudes of people in His ministry, and at one time, He preached to more than 5,000 people without a sound system. Jesus would declare the works of the kingdom of God, and masses of people would follow Him. Yet, Jesus consistently chose to focus on individuals amid the multitude.

Time and time again, in Jesus' Earthly ministry, He would concentrate His complete attention on one person, engaging with that individual as if they were the only person in the world. You would be astonished when you read the gospels to notice how many times Jesus cut through the crowd, found the one, and ministered to them. From the Parable of the Lost Son, we recognize that when one person is saved, great joy is released in heaven. But I contend that when one person is saved, not only is great joy released in heaven, but great potential also is released on Earth.

When one person is saved, not only is great joy released in heaven, but great potential also is released on Earth.

Mark shares an account of when Jesus said to His disciples, "Let us go over to the other side," referring to the other side of Galilee (4:35). Jesus and His followers climbed into a boat and began to sail through a raging storm, heading for the other side of Galilee to a place called the Decapolis. Jesus' primary ministry had been in Capernaum, but He traveled through the night and the storm to reach this area called Gadara, which was part of the Decapolis. Decapolis meant "Ten Cities," named for the ten Gentile, Greek-influenced cities in the region that spanned the entire east side of the Sea of Galilee. During the storm on the way to Decapolis, Jesus fell asleep in the rear of the boat. The disciples frantically awakened Jesus and asked Him, "Don't You care we are perishing?" Jesus got up, stepped to the bow of the boat, and commanded, "Peace be still!" Immediately, the storm ceased, and the boat arrived on the shore of Gadara in the Decapolis.

When they arrived in this strange region, the disciples must have been thinking, "Why are we here? I hope this trip is worth losing a night's sleep and fighting through the storm."

Not long after stepping out of the boat, Jesus looked across the seashore to see an unclothed man running toward Him. Can you imagine the looks on the disciples' bewildered faces? As the naked, disheveled man, with scars all over his body and crazy eyes, ran toward Jesus, he was screaming, "Leave me alone! What do you want with me?" Jesus authoritatively spoke to the demon, saying, "Come out of this man, you impure spirit!" At that moment, Jesus asked the evil spirit, "What is your name?" The man, completely overtaken by evil, screamed out, "My name is Legion, for we are many." The demons pleaded with Jesus not to send them out of the region and asked to be sent into a herd of pigs. "Send us among the pigs; allow us to go into them" (cf. Mark 5:1–12). (Decapolis was a gentile region, so raising pigs was a lucrative business. Eating pork was not only allowed but was also encouraged.)

Jesus agreed to their request and cast the demons out of the man into a drove of pigs. The grazing herd, about two thousand in number, became rabid, ran off a cliff into the lake, and drowned. What a dramatic, astounding encounter! The man was now in his right mind, free from demonic oppression. Realizing his indecency, he dressed and then sat down at the feet of Jesus to hear what his new Master had to say.

When the people of the Decapolis saw what happened and discovered that this wild, graveyard-dwelling man, who could not be contained, was now healed and in his right mind, they did not rejoice. Rather than being thrilled, they were afraid and possibly even angry because their livelihood ran off a cliff and died. Years of bacon and ham cultivation were lost in a moment. They were so upset that they pleaded with Jesus to leave their region.

At their request, Jesus boarded the small fishing vessel with His disciples for the return trip to Capernaum on the other side of Galilee. The man, who was delivered, begged to go with Him. Jesus responded, "No. You can't go with Me. Go home to your people and tell them how much the Lord has done for you and how He has had mercy on you." Scripture says this man went throughout the Decapolis declaring what Jesus had done in his life.[31]

When we step back and look at this biblical narrative, Jesus appears to have taken His entire ministry team, with all the associated expenses, through a difficult, storm-tossed, night journey across the Sea of Galilee to find and save just one, demon-possessed man.

Why? Why would Jesus go to all of this trouble, effort, and expense for one crazy man, who was the scourge of his community? Was it because Jesus is willing to do whatever it takes to save one? Yes! His heart is always restless, looking for the lost one, and His death on the cross proves He will do whatever it takes to rescue us. So, the trip across the Sea of Galilee was absolutely a rescue mission for ONE.

However, Jesus also knew that by reaching this one man, He would unlock the man's potential to make a difference. He instructed him to share his story, scars and all. The people of Gadara and the Decapolis must have been amazed. The former graveyard-dwelling, flesh-cutting, demoniac was now wearing clothes, talking sensibly, and proclaiming that he was free because of the ministry of Jesus of Nazareth. Jesus knew that the power of this one man's testimony would make a profound impact. Testimonies always do! Hearing from a man who once was possessed by a legion of devils would change the Gadarenes' attitude regarding Jesus' ministry and the atmosphere of the Decapolis.

A short time later, we witness this transformation. Mark reports: "Then Jesus left the vicinity of Tyre and went through Sidon, down to the Sea of Galilee and into the region of the Decapolis. There some people brought to

Him a man who was deaf and could hardly talk, and they begged Jesus to place His hand on him" (7:31–33). Do you see the difference?

In Mark Chapter 5, after Jesus delivers the demon-possessed man, the people of Decapolis beg Him to leave them alone. In Chapter 7, they beg Jesus to perform His ministry among them. Two chapters. What changed? The difference was the consistent, widespread testimony of the man from the graveyard. When they asked (and even when they didn't ask), he would share that Jesus changed his life and set him free. The Decapolis was opened to Jesus' ministry through the power of One man's witness. Never underestimate someone's potential for good, even if they are presently a self-destructing, graveyard streaker.

INTENTIONAL DETOUR

The Mediterranean sun beat down on the disciples. It was time for lunch. Frustration was building with their Samarian detour, so perhaps a hearty meal would encourage the team. At least, it might if they could find some good Jewish food in such a strange place. It was difficult to understand why Jesus chose the road through Samaria. The normal route for the Jews between Judea and Galilee was through the Jordan Valley. This was to avoid contact with the Samaritans, whom the Jewish people considered enemies.

The Samaritans were a mixture of Gentile and Jew, and for many years were rejected by the Jews, who at times called them dogs or half-breeds. This animosity began with the division of Israel into the northern and southern kingdoms, following the reign of Solomon. The hostility increased during the days of Nehemiah and Ezra as the Samaritans resisted the rebuilding of the temple and the wall around Jerusalem. Through the years, the division continued to deepen. The Samaritans had their worship system and their holy mountain, and they accepted only the first five books of Scripture (the Pentateuch) as authoritative. Jews refused to have contact with the Samaritans; therefore, Jesus' decision to travel through Samaria was difficult for the disciples to understand. The normal route through the Jordan Valley would have been nicer and easier. Climbing the Samaritan hills was a lot of work. It just didn't make sense to go through this spiritually desolate place. Who wanted to be around Samaritans anyway?

Apparently, Jesus wanted to be around Samaritans—or at least, He wanted to meet with one unique Samaritan. In retrospect, the entire route through Samaria seemed to be designed precisely in a way to encounter one lady who needed God. Once again, Jesus would concentrate

His ministry on one person and thus unlock exponential potential among the masses.

Jesus sat on a well while His team went for lunch. There He encountered a Samaritan woman. Her understanding of worship and God's chosen people was different from Jesus' disciples. Beyond her religious background, she struggled relationally. She had been married to five different men and was now living with a man who was not her husband. Relational dysfunction was her difficult norm.

During biblical times, the law allowed a man to divorce his wife at his discretion, leaving her economically, physically, and psychologically vulnerable. If a woman upset her husband enough to provoke a divorce, she had no power to resist or decline it, and she was not granted the same right to divorce him.[32] This woman at the well, in essence, represents those brokenhearted, wounded people in our world who are incessantly coping with rejection and abandonment, looking for something in other people that humans are not able to supply. Broken, empty, used, abandoned, and ashamed, this woman approached Jacob's well all alone that day.

Jesus spoke first. "Please give Me a drink."

The woman was amazed. "You are a Jew, and I am a Samaritan," she quipped out loud. These differences, along with the fact that Jesus was a man and she was a woman traveling alone, meant that for Him (especially as a rabbi) to address her was totally out of the social norm. Even more noteworthy was that He engaged in a theological discussion with a Samaritan woman in broad daylight for all to see. If we are not careful, we read quickly through this familiar narrative and miss one more very significant moment. This was the first time Jesus revealed to anyone that He was the Messiah! And He shared this life-transforming truth with a lonely, social outcast by a well in a despised region of the world.

At that moment, Jesus stepped over social and religious boundaries to reach a hurting heart. Although this was socially abnormal, a Savior pursuing His broken creation was completely within God's spiritual norm. Jesus offered her a spring of living water that would remain inside her and overflow to eternal life. She wanted this water. She wanted her heart to be satisfied. She wanted to break the cycle of dysfunction and abandonment. She wanted to be whole and live in peace, knowing she was loved by Someone who would never leave her or forsake her. She wanted eternal life. Her encounter with the Messiah would change her forever and would open the door of revival to the Samaritan people.

Her taste of the living water, coupled with Jesus' spiritual insight, convinced the woman that she had met the Messiah. The man at the well was the deliverer from heaven. Even Samaritans could get excited about that.

She left her water pot immediately and went into the city to share the news of her discovery. "Come, see a man who told me everything I ever did. Could this be the Messiah?" (John 4:29). Her message impacted the multitudes. Many Samaritans left the city and made their way toward the well for their encounter with Jesus. For the next two days, Jesus ministered to the Samaritans, and many became believers.

One relationally dysfunctional woman's singular encounter with Jesus was the key to reaching a large number of Samaritans. Heaven rejoiced that this lost lady was found, and the Earth was blessed as the potential within her was released. Jesus did it again—He focused on one, and the masses were reached.

IT'S NOT OVER UNTIL IT'S OVER

The nightmare was ending. Lives filled with failure and sin were coming to a dreadful end. Crucifixion was the sentence, and the cruel reality of the cross was settling upon them.

Hanging between heaven and Earth were two men whose sentences matched their crimes of murder and robbery (Luke 23). The morning execution lingered into the afternoon as only crucifixion could. Adding insult to injury were the multitudes passing by to witness the pain. Actually, three people were crucified that day. Two were thieves, and one was a King—He was called the King of the Jews.

One of the thieves made fun of this King by taunting Him and demanding that He save Himself and rescue them from this moment. This thief's lack of regret and remorse coursed out of his bitter heart. He would use his last breaths the way he had lived, in cursing and anger.

The other thief, however, was experiencing something very different. As his breaths drew shallower, his regret seemed to grow deeper. He knew that Jesus the King was being crucified because of envy and had committed no crime. A victim of his failures, he was now hanging beside the Holy One. The end was coming quickly. His life raced before him like a high-speed movie. The early struggles in his quest for survival had turned sour, and he found himself breaking rule after rule. As the years passed, his heart grew out of control as if some strange force entrapped him until the darkness was overwhelming. He had never wanted to end up this way. Yes, he deserved to die, and he knew it, yet, he wished things could have been different. Now, feeling as though his chest cavity would explode out of his exhausted and emaciated body, his hope was gone. He couldn't go back and relive his life. It was over, he was condemned, death was imminent, and hope was forever lost . . . or was it?

The King hanging beside him was being killed unjustly. He had heard the crowd chant for Barabbas to be released and Jesus to be crucified. He had watched this King of the Jews endure beating and berating without any bitterness. And, he had just heard this same King forgive all those who were perpetrating His unjust death. Not only was the King hanging beside him holy, but He also had the power to forgive. Maybe, the King would forgive him. Maybe God was providing him an opportunity for hope at the end of his nightmare life. Maybe, just maybe, he could be saved.

Realizing that this King's kingdom was different, the repenting thief said: "Jesus, remember me when You come into Your Kingdom."

Jesus' answer revealed His heart: "Truly I tell you, today you will be with me in paradise" (v. 43). Wow! The thief's trajectory changed immediately from a hopeless life to eternal life with one profound confession of Jesus as Lord! That day, the nightmare turned into an everlasting dream come true. The thief was saved.

Jesus did it again. Oh, what a Savior! Despite the passion of the cross, the weight of every sinner's sin crushing His body, and the demons of hell attacking His spirit, Jesus once again took time for the ONE. While dying, He focused ministry on one man, and because of this, He reached millions.

I am convinced that the testimony of the dying thief who repented with his last breaths has served to lead more people to receive Jesus Christ and be saved from destruction than any other account in Scripture. Millions of people will be in heaven because, at the very end of their life, someone shared with them this story about a thief who—at the end of his life—turned to Jesus and received eternal life. This story gives them hope that "If He forgave the thief hanging beside Him, He can also forgive me."

In the end, millions will be in heaven because of one. Jesus' ministry to the thief on the cross and his subsequent salvation released a harvest among the dying for centuries to come.

THE POWER OF ONE
PATTERN CONTINUES

This pattern of one person being reached and subsequently releasing a harvest for multitudes continued in the early church.

Philip was in the midst of one of the great outpourings described by Luke in The Acts of the Apostles. The disciples were in Samaria, and people were being healed, touched, filled with the Holy Spirit, and delivered from demonic possession. At the crescendo of this spiritual high, the Lord said to Philip, "I want you to leave this revival and go to the desert."

Undoubtedly, Philip said, "What? Are You kidding? This is the greatest revival that has happened since Jesus was resurrected!" Yet the Holy Spirit reaffirmed, "I know, but I want you to go to the desert." So, Philip left the multitude and traveled south on the road toward Gaza. When he got to the desert, he noticed an Ethiopian man reading Scripture while riding in a chariot. The man was a prominent leader in the Ethiopian Queen Candace's administration. Philip joined the man and explained that the words of the prophet Isaiah he was studying were prophesying about the suffering servant, Jesus. The Ethiopian not only received the gospel with gladness but also was baptized in water on the spot.[33] This converted Ethiopian official became the first person to bring the good news of Jesus as the Savior to Africa.

Today, the African continent has more than 667 million Christians living there—more than any other continent in the world![34] God sent Philip to one, and this one person, ultimately, released a harvest across the entire African continent.

Peter preached the gospel to one man, Cornelius, and his family. This Spirit-empowered encounter opened the way for Gentiles to receive Christ.

One European man appeared to Paul in a vision while he was in Troas, and in the vision, pleaded with Paul, "Come over to Macedonia and help us" (Acts 16:9). This call by one man in a vision motivated Paul's entire missionary team to cross the Aegean Sea and to take the good news of Jesus to Europe. One Philippian jailer was saved in the middle of the night, and Christianity was established on the continent of Europe. From Europe, the good news then spread to the entire world.

And then there's the example of Paul himself. Jesus intentionally encountered Saul of Tarsus—the zealous, misguided Hebrew—while he was traveling to Damascus on a mission to persecute Christians. Christ's light was brighter than the noonday sun, and with a voice clearer than thunder, He changed Saul the Christian antagonist to Paul the Christian ambassador. Even from heaven, Jesus continued His method of finding and focusing His ministry attention on one person. Heaven rejoiced, and the Earth was changed as this one person's potential was released. Paul would become the most prolific missionary and leader of the early church. He wrote a large portion of the New Testament, and 2,000 years later, his work continues to dramatically impact the world.

ONE PERSON AT A TIME

Remember the story of Cameron Townsend, who received the charge to go to the Bibleless people of the world? That one man, with a burden for those without God's Word, surrendered to the call of God on his life and has made a profound impact on the Earth.

In 1942, Townsend founded Wycliffe Bible Translators, one of the world's most significant missionary forces. Wycliffe has been a part of translating the Scriptures into thousands of minority languages, bringing God's Word to millions in their native tongue or heart language. Wycliff is part of an alliance of Bible Agencies that is on track to see a Bible translated in every language—all 6,000+ of them—by 2033. What an impact![35]

Looking back on Townsends' time with the Cakchiquel of Guatemala, one more story is worth noting. Not long after Townsend arrived in Guatemala, he met a Cakchiquel man named Silverio, who knew a little Spanish. When he was first given a Spanish Bible, he could read some but grew frustrated over the many words he did not understand. Silverio had been involved in idol worship and rituals and was far from God. Townsend ministered to Silverio, and as he learned God's Word, he was converted. Following his salvation, he burned his idols, saying, "I served them all my life. I thought it was time they served me, so I made kindling wood out of them and cooked my beans."[36]

The impact Townsend made on Silverio's life did not stop with him. Just six months after receiving Jesus, this man, Silverio, led forty other Cakchiquel people to Christ![37] The gospel continued to spread among the people.

Townsend's reaching one man with the gospel unlocked a multitude and brought a harvest to an entire people group. Reaching the multitudes always begins by reaching ONE!

THE BUTTERFLY EFFECT ACROSS THE GENERATIONS

In 1855, a Sunday school teacher named Edward Kimball led a seventeen-year-old shoe clerk named Dwight L. Moody to Christ. D. L. Moody began a ministry that reached millions of people, and in one service, he preached and awakened the heart of a young pastor named F. B. Meyer, who then preached on college campuses.

One of Meyer's converts was Wilbur Chapman. After attending a D. L. Moody campaign, Chapman became

Moody's co-worker and hired an ex-baseball player, Billy Sunday, to be his assistant. Sunday became a great evangelist and held crusades across America, including in Charlotte, North Carolina. A group of local businessmen in Charlotte were touched by Sunday's ministry and began praying for greater local outreach. They invited a minister by the name of Mordecai Ham to preach at a tent meeting in Charlotte in 1934.

On November 1, 1934, during the tent meeting, a sixteen-year-old boy came forward to receive Christ. That sixteen-year-old boy was Billy Graham,[38] who became one of the most effective evangelists of all time, seeing more than two million people respond to the invitation to receive Christ at his crusades.[39]

And where did it all start? With a Sunday School teacher reaching one.

Yes, when one person is saved, there is rejoicing in heaven! But a dramatic, tangible, and powerful potential on Earth is also released. I believe God is calling us to live like Jesus and focus on the ONE. And if we will focus on the one, He will unlock the multitudes.

CHAPTER 4

THE RE-PERSONALIZATION OF THE GREAT COMMISSION

The world has significantly changed since Billy Graham first received Christ, and society continues to dramatically shift. Due to technological innovations, cultural changes are happening at a rate faster than ever before in history, and the world, as we know it, is constantly fluctuating.

If you were to walk into any crowded public space today, what would you see? Years ago, before the release of the first iPhone in 2007, you may have seen total strangers chatting among themselves, a variety of conversations taking place. Now, the picture is quite different. More often than not, you'll find people silently staring down at their devices instead of engaging with one another. This may even be true at your dinner table—if you still have one!

Board a flight and sit down. What do you hear? For the most part, silence. It used to be customary to introduce yourself to the passenger sitting next to you and ask questions like: "Where are you from?" and "Where are you going?" Now, it is quite common to avoid talking altogether, putting on a personal headset, and raising the invisible "no communication" wall while focusing on your device.

These everyday life scenarios underscore the rise of individualism in our world and the growing tendency toward self-absorption. Individualism is defined as a "doctrine that the interests of the individual are or ought to be ethically paramount," and it is at an all-time high. Just look around at the myriad of customized products, subscription boxes, workout and meal plans, curated music playlists, and shopping experiences—you name it—and they are all growing in popularity. People desire to have their wants and needs met and are willing to pay a high price to achieve that.

Ross Douthat wrote in an article in the March 2014, *New York Times:* "In the future, it seems there will only be one 'ism—Individualism—and its rule will never end."[40] Research examining fifty-one years of data on individualist practices and values across seventy-eight countries found individualism is on the rise globally.[41]

You may say, *"This is terrible news if we are trying to reach everyone!"* Yes, but even though we have reasons to be concerned, I also believe we have a reason for much hope:

> **Behind the headphones, devices, and unique trends lies a generation that can completely change the world.**

Behind the headphones, devices, and unique trends lies a generation that can completely change the world.

THE MOST INDIVIDUALISTIC GENERATION EVER

The generation born roughly between 1995 and 2015 is known as Generation Z, and it is the largest generation on Earth. It is comprised of almost three billion people, which is more than thirty percent of the world's total population.[42] The generation is also key to the conversation about reaching every person on Earth with the message of Jesus. Yet, this dynamic group of young people is the most individualistic generation in history.[43] They are creative, entrepreneurial, technologically savvy, racially diverse, globally connected, industrious, and passionate about changing the world. While this individuality may have some negative components, it also has positives and ultimately will impact the way Generation Z connects with God and how the generation views the truth that each person has individual access to Him.

In this world of growing individualism, Generation Z wants to be noticed, understood, and known. This social phenomenon is marked by high self-expression, self-reliance, and personal autonomy. They are in the business of trading traditional norms and societal expectations for their uniqueness. They want to be uniquely valued for the people they are and not the category they can be clustered into.

"I'm not my family, I'm not my friends, I'm not my school, I'm not my city, I'm not my country," says Generation Z. "Don't put me in a box—see *me.*"

Previous generations may have believed something because their parents believed it or their community accepted it. Generation Z is quite different. In the age of information overload, they are bombarded with an onslaught of persuasive movements, brands, and ideologies from around the world, all clamoring for their attention and allegiance in a way no previous generation has ever had to navigate. More information has led to more questions for this generation, and presented with a multitude of ideas, they are capable of customizing and curating their lives and their belief systems. They are uniquely positioned to ask powerful questions and push the boundaries of understanding.

In their quest for individuality, Generation Z is crying out to be noticed, and if we are going to reach this generation, we must focus on them as individuals. The pandemic incubated this individualism, transforming them into the most introverted generation ever. At Oral Roberts University, where I serve, we have noticed this significant shift. New students are generally not as outgoing as those who have attended the university previously. Today's young person is much quieter, more timid, and more reserved. Because of this shift, previous methods that worked in reaching prior generations may not work for Generation Z. While the Millennial Generation before them often traveled in groups and could be influenced by their friends, Generation Z is different, and reaching them is going to require an individualized approach.

At the same time Generation Z is crying out to be noticed, they are also crying out on behalf of their peers in determination to stand against injustices. In his article, "10 Characteristics of Generation Z," Shane Pruitt writes, "Generation Z is globally minded and want their life to matter. They are fully aware of their imperfections, evil, hate, and injustices. They are looking for solutions, answers, and impact. They're not scared to die young; however, they are terrified to die at a ripe-old age and have done nothing significant with their lives in their own age."[44]

THE GREATEST INJUSTICE

Despite their tendency to be introverted, Generation Z is not afraid to stand up against injustice and make their life count. They are not hesitant to make their voices heard on issues that matter most to them. Issues important to Generation Z include health care, mental health, higher education, economic security, civic engagement, racial equity, and the environment.[45] They want to make a difference in their world and the lives of the vulnerable.

While all these issues need to be addressed, I contend that the greatest injustice in the world is that we have the means, the money, the mechanisms, the technology, and the power to share the good news of Jesus with every person on Earth, yet many *still* have never heard about Him and are on their way to an eternity separated from God.

The Joshua Project estimates 3.36 billion people are unreached.[46] If we can help Generation Z capture the depth of this injustice and commit to acting against it, then we will see a massive movement focused on bringing Christ to those who have never heard the gospel and righting the greatest injustice of our time. Can you imagine the potential of a passionate generation using technology and creativity to share Jesus with individuals all over the world? The impact will be massive!

How do we reach an introverted world? One person at a time.

I believe God is calling today's church to re-personalize the Great Commission and once again focus on individual people. Generation Z is positioned with the worldview, self-understanding, and technological skills to lead the way in this new era of evangelism. They will be the greatest contemporary force in bringing the good news of Jesus to everyone on Earth.

COME AND SEE

The gospel writer John recounts a moment when one of Jesus' disciples discovered he is personally known and seen by God, and he gives us a further glimpse into God's heart for individuals. Jesus found Philip after leaving Galilee and called Philip to follow Him (John 1:43). Subsequently, Philip found Nathanael and told him about Jesus: "We have found the one Moses wrote about in the Law, and about whom the prophets also wrote—Jesus of Nazareth, the son of Joseph" (v. 45).

At that proclamation, Nathanael, who was taken aback and pessimistic about this possibility, exclaimed, "There is no way the Messiah could come from Nazareth! Can anything good come from there?" Philip, who I imagine was full of great excitement, invited Nathanael, "Come and see" (v. 46).

While Nathanael was on his way, Jesus approached him and complimented what He saw in Nathanael: "Behold an Israelite indeed, in whom is no guile!" (John 1:47, KJV). Hearing this compliment, Nathanael wondered how Jesus knew him. With that statement, Jesus was calling out the best in Nathanael. This made him receptive to what Jesus had to say next: "I know you, Nathanael. I saw you while you were still under the fig tree before Philip called you."

The fig tree represented Israel but could also represent a place of reflection and contemplation. Isaiah, the prophet, wrote that the day would come when every Israelite home would have its own fig tree—a place of rest and a place to meditate on God. Jesus was saying to Nathanael, "As you were sitting under the fig tree, contemplating the things of God and the coming Messiah, I saw you and your pure heart." Astounded, Nathanael declared, "Rabbi, you are the

Son of God; you are the king of Israel!" (v. 49). He was the first person in Scripture to make this proclamation.

Many times, when we come to Jesus, much like Nathanael, the revelation of who we are astounds us and draws us into a relationship with Him. Jesus reveals that we are seen and known, and He invites us to come and see ourselves the way He does.

One of our greatest human desires and perhaps needs— is to be fully known and loved. This desire has escalated in Generation Z. Tied to the effects of social media while living in a world with more than eight billion other human beings, this generation has become fragile and needs to be validated and feel accepted.

With a renewed focus on the individual, we can invite a generation to come and see that they are truly known by God. "God sees you. He knows everything about you. He sees your joy and sorrow, your passion and pain. He loves you and has a great plan for your life. He loves you so much that He sent His Son Jesus to die on the cross for *you*, and He is inviting you to personally know Him and be saved."

If we can align our hearts with this truth and allow God to help us see individuals the way He does, we can reach an entire generation and the world!

A NEW WAY FOR A NEW DAY

Generation Z is a unique generation living in a unique time in history. The combination of these two forces could be catalytic for the greatest evangelistic thrust known to man. COVID-19 brought forth an unprecedented sequence of changes in the fabric of nations, communities, and churches. The shift from the industrialized age paradigm to that of the digital age has forced the church to learn the language, values, and communication streams of this generation. It has invited the church to become increasingly adaptable and nimble in its operations, moving from a gathering mindset into an individual-focused approach.

God has gifted His body with immense creativity, and He has inspired resourcefulness that goes far beyond what takes place within the four walls of a church. One clear example of this is the YouVersion Bible app.

Founded by Bobby Gruenewald in 2008 (one year after the release of the iPhone), YouVersion has wielded the power of technology to place God's Word into the hands of people worldwide and help them engage more consistently with Scripture. The app was one of the first 200 free apps available when Apple launched the App Store in July 2008.[47] Offering more than 2,800 Bible versions in more than 1,800 languages, it has been downloaded on more than 500 million devices in every country around the world.[48] What an unprecedented impact!

Another example of creative evangelism in our day is through the hit series *The Chosen*, which is about the Earthly life and ministry of Jesus. Through an innovative and captivating story-telling approach, *The Chosen*—available to watch for free and on major streaming sites—has garnered an audience of over 100 million viewers and aims to reach one billion viewers worldwide.[49] Some parts of the series have been translated into seventy languages, and the Come and See Foundation has plans for the series to become available in up to 600 languages.[50] Around the world, by the click of a button, those who may never darken the doors of a church or open a Bible can now engage with the message of Jesus through a television show. We are living in times the early church could have only dreamed about! Technological advances are making it possible to reach everyone on Earth, and we

> **Technological advances are making it possible to reach everyone on Earth, and we are positioned in an unprecedented moment in history to do so.**

are positioned in an unprecedented moment in history to do so.

As the COVID-19 coronavirus surfaced onto the world stage in January 2020, churches around the globe found themselves in the throes of disruption. With government-imposed restrictions on public gatherings, urging—or even requiring—believers to set aside assembling and to remain within the confines of their homes for the sake of the greater good, pastors had to face the uncertainty of what would become of their congregations. ORU was not spared from the disruption as our once bustling classrooms transformed into remote, virtual spaces where students and instructors navigated the new education terrain in a changed world. In the middle of it all, I often asked God, "What do You want to do during this time?" I felt He was saying: "I am initiating a new way for a new day."

When indoor church services were closed, parking lot and drive-by church services opened. When prayer meetings were stopped, prayer caravans around hospitals and medical care centers intensified. When the community was restricted, online church engagement grew to an all-time high. While not a substitute for in-person gatherings, seeing the creative energy of the Holy Spirit moving in ministries to operate in brand-new ways was amazing.

In the wake of the pandemic, God moved the church to a new level of effectiveness. A new way for a new day was required for us to continue ministering. While I don't believe God sent the pandemic that took the lives of many and caused so much suffering, I believe He has used it to highlight how He is moving on the Earth.

As we transition into the post-pandemic era, I firmly believe we are poised at the precipice of the most remarkable surge of evangelism ever witnessed in human history, fueled by a fresh and powerful outpouring of the Holy Spirit. The pandemic has accomplished something unprecedented in the past century. It has touched every corner of the globe, reaching every nation, every culture, and every family. Even a nuclear bomb, though it would shake the Earth, would not necessarily affect the whole world. But the pandemic has impacted even the most secluded islands that believed they were safe.

What is amazing to think about is if you clustered together every single one of the individual COVID-19 viruses, they would barely fill a large can,[51] yet their influence has been felt worldwide. Not even World War II had such a universal impact. Lives in every part of the globe were shaken and some were even devastated by the pandemic.

Worldwide, people need fresh hope. I believe God is using this moment in history to prepare the way for a new hunger to know the living God, the Healer, and resurrected One who conquered death on the cross and can conquer death in our lives. If something as small as the COVID-19 virus can shake the whole world, how much more can the gospel of Jesus Christ make an impact once it has reached every corner of the Earth?

If we can tap into this move of God and make His passion our own, we will be part of the greatest revival in the history of the world.

We now know this reach is possible. A new hunger is dawning on the Earth. A fresh fire is stirring within a new generation, and a new wave of global evangelization is swelling. If we can tap into this move of God and make His passion our own, we will be part of the greatest revival in the history of the world.

TO ONE AND ALL

While walking with the disciples through the Mount of Olives toward Gethsemane, Jesus assured them they would reconnect where it all started after His resurrection. He said, "But after I have risen, I will go ahead of you into Galilee."

They were concluding three years full of lessons, miracles, and wonder, yet nothing could have prepared them for that night in the garden and that day at Golgotha as they witnessed Jesus die a criminal's death on the cross. The disciples were now scattered and afraid.

On Sunday, Mary Magdalene burst into the room, affirming that the Savior had risen. She had seen Him, and He was alive! Peter and John rushed to the scene only to find an empty grave and strips of linen.

On the same day, Jesus joined two disciples walking toward Emmaus and broke bread with them. He later joined the ten, showing His wounded hands and feet, so they would believe. However, one of the disciples was missing, so a week later, Jesus passed through locked doors, again looking for the one—Thomas. During the next forty days, Jesus revealed Himself to more than 500 believers. He also came by the shores of the Sea of Galilee, where He prepared breakfast for seven of His disciples, filled their empty nets with 153 large fish, and finished His pending conversation with Peter about whether he really loved Him. Jesus appeared to His brother, James, and then to all the apostles.

These men had followed Jesus for three years throughout the regions of Galilee, Judea, Samaria, and the Roman Decapolis, listening to Him preach and perform signs and wonders. More than followers, they were friends. They had watched Him subdue the powers of nature by the sound of His voice and felt His power in their hands through the multiplication of bread and fish—all because He said so. They were standing now with hopeful anticipation that the world they believed would come into existence had finally arrived. They believed He could and would make it happen. He was the One!

"Is Jesus going to finally launch a revolution as Joshua did, who led the Israelites to conquer the Promised Land?"

"Is He going to use His might to overthrow the Roman government like when He sent the ten plagues to free Israel from Egypt?"

"Is He going to unleash His wisdom and dismantle the self-righteous rule of the Pharisees?"

"Is He going to arm us with supernatural power like He did Samson to fight the Philistines?"

"Is He finally going to establish His kingdom?"

The answer to these final questions was, in fact, yes—but not in the way they expected. Each gospel writer recorded a different angle and focus of what Jesus said on the mountain that day. After His words, He ascended into the heavens while the disciples descended to their mission on Earth, ignited with new passion and purpose.

Matthew, the most analytical of Jesus' disciples, wrote for a largely Jewish audience and from a Jewish perspective. He recounted Jesus' words: "All authority in heaven and on earth has been given to me. Therefore, go and make disciples of all nations, baptizing them in the name of the Father and of the Son and of the Holy Spirit, and teaching them to obey everything I have commanded you. And surely, I am with you always, to the very end of the age" (28:18–20).

Luke, the educated researcher, historian, and doctor who wrote for a mostly Greek-educated audience and the courts of Rome, penned: "This is what is written: The Messiah will suffer and rise from the dead on the third day, and repentance for the forgiveness of sins will be preached in his name to all nations, beginning at Jerusalem" (24:46–47). As the author of the book of Acts, Luke further recorded Jesus saying, "But you will receive power when the Holy Spirit comes on you; and you will be my witnesses in Jerusalem, and in all Judea and Samaria, and to the ends of the earth" (1:8).

John, who took a spiritualized approach to his gospel, recorded: "'Peace be with you! As the Father has sent me, I am sending you.' And with that, he breathed on them and said, 'Receive the Holy Spirit'" (20:21–22).

And then, we have Mark's gospel. A common man of the Roman world, Mark wrote an action-packed account for Gentiles, who would not have understood Jewish customs. His writing is more like a series of newspaper articles—short, concise, to the point, and answering the basic questions of who, what, where, when, and how. When Mark related his version of the Great Commission that Christ had given them, he wrote: "Go into all the world and preach the gospel to all creation. Whoever believes and is baptized will be saved, but whoever does not believe will be condemned" (16:15–16). The New King James Version translates verse fifteen in this way: "Go into all the world and preach the gospel to every creature." Another translation chooses this way to say it: "Go everywhere and announce the message of God's good news to one and all" (MSG).

With this one imperative, Christ encapsulated His assignment for the disciples. The last three years had been full of preaching, teaching, miracles, ministry to the crowds, and profound encounters with individuals. Yet, these final instructions were His ultimate request—reach everyone. EveryONE!

The key is understanding the Greek words for "every creature," which are *pas* and *ktisis*. *Pas* is defined as "each, every, any, all, the whole, everyone, all things, everything."

Ktisis is defined as "of individual things, beings, a creature, a creation." In the context of Mark's writing, these two words communicate the literal idea of preaching the gospel to every individual being and creature on Earth.

Some scholars will note that Mark's account of the Great Commission is not verifiably included in the earliest copies of his gospel. This may be true, but regardless, the truth of what these verses communicate is ingrained throughout the rest of his gospel and the New Testament. Following are clear examples that the good news about Jesus Christ is for Every One.

"Because we have our hope set on the living God, who is the Savior of *all people*, especially of those who believe" (1 Timothy 4:10, ESV, emphasis added).

"The Lord is not slow in keeping his promise, as some understand slowness. Instead, he is patient with you, not wanting anyone to perish, but *everyone* to come to repentance" (2 Peter 3:9, emphasis added).

"The Spirit and the bride say, 'Come!' And let the one who hears say, 'Come!' Let the one who is thirsty come; and let the one who wishes take the free gift of the water of life" (Revelation 22:17).

"For *whosoever* shall call upon the name of the Lord shall be saved" (Romans 10:13, KJV, emphasis added).

These verses, and many more, reinforce that though not everyone will accept the gospel, everyone has been invited by God to receive salvation through Jesus. God's heart and salvation are not for a select group of people but for everyONE.

As followers of Jesus, we should embrace this fact as the driving mission of our lives. Yes, let's take the gospel to every nation. Let's nurture His message in every ethnicity and culture, and let's disciple believers for spiritual growth. Let's plant churches and witness revival. But above all, our primary focus must remain fixed on our greatest priority, which is leading men, women, boys, and girls all over the world to Jesus Christ until each individual has had an opportunity to know Him. With a growing population, this work will never be finished. The world population grows by 200,000 every single day.[52] We are called to live Great Commandment lifestyles with the Great Commission goal of reaching everyone.

> **Our primary focus must remain fixed on our greatest priority.**

I celebrate the wonderful Spiritual activities taking place within the church. I deeply cherish worship, Bible studies, and prayer sessions. And, of course, as president of Oral Roberts University, I believe in education and equipping leaders for kingdom impact. So many good things are happening in the Lord's work that it would be easy to miss the most important focus of all—people. Our crucial need is to rekindle our zeal for individuals and their eternal destiny. Jesus exhibited this kind of lifestyle. He addressed the crowds, established the church, rebuked heresy, healed the sick, broke the power of demons, and consistently taught the truth, but He never overlooked the potential impact of a single individual coming to know Him as Savior. Sharing Jesus with people should be the most consistently prioritized passion and practice for believers. It should be as easy as ABC.

AS EASY AS ABC

In the 1990s, I took my first trip to China—a place I had been longing to visit for some time. I went with a Christian tour group but was also able to tape our first two episodes of *World Impact with Billy Wilson*. We saw the sites of China and even met with famous Chinese Christian leaders. Yet, the best part of the trip was not on the agenda.

Our trip around Beijing was incredible, and we saw everything we could have wanted to see—the Great Wall, the Summer Palace, and Tiananmen Square. Throughout the trip, we had an incredible tour guide, a young lady named Hong.

Hong spoke decent English, and along the way, our team talked to her about Jesus. I asked about her religion and background, learned of her beliefs, and shared my own. On the last morning of the trip, the Holy Spirit impressed on me strongly: "You have made a friend in Hong on this trip. She is a wonderful lady and has been kind to you. It's time to tell her about Me and invite her to know Me."

Hong rode with us on the bus back to the airport, and the ride through Beijing traffic was long. I took advantage of the time we had together, pulled out a paper napkin, and began writing the English letters A-B-C. Hong's English was limited, but I felt she would understand the simplicity of ABC. I bent down on my knees in front of her and for the next ten minutes, began sharing the gospel, telling Hong that Jesus, the One we'd been talking about, is real, and knowing Him is easy—as easy as ABC!

Ask Him to forgive your sins and come into your heart.

Believe that Jesus died for your sins and that God raised Him from the dead.

Confess that He is Lord.

If she did these three simple steps of Asking, Believing, and Confessing—she would be saved. Hong began to cry, and right there on our way to Beijing airport, she gave her heart to Jesus. It was an amazing moment. For some time, we kept in touch with Hong, who had a vibrant faith, but as often happens in China, we eventually lost track of her.

Fast forward a few years, and once again, I was visiting China. This time I was representing ORU. We had with us a gentleman whom I will refer to as Bob for the sake of privacy. He was a multi-millionaire and helped open doors for us with the Chinese government. Because of Bob's help, we met with the head of the Chinese Department of Education and ultimately obtained a preferred status for ORU. At the time of this writing, we have memorandums of understanding with more than ten universities in China, and several dozen Chinese students are now studying at our university. Thank you, Bob!

As we were about to leave Beijing, the Lord began speaking to me about Bob. He had become a friend and a real blessing to our group on the trip. It was the last day I was going to see him, and while I was in the shower, the Lord spoke to me, "Use your napkin." I was confused for a while until it finally dawned on me: the ABCs.

I met our group for breakfast in the hotel restaurant where Bob would be joining us. I had an ink pen with me, but no paper. To my surprise, the Marriott Hotel restaurant, which had previously only used cloth napkins during breakfast, had switched to paper napkins on this particular morning. Amazing! After eating breakfast, I sat down beside Bob, grabbed a napkin, and asked him, "May I share something with you?" Because we had become friends, he agreed without hesitation.

It is as easy as ABC: Ask, Believe, Confess.

I began writing the ABCs of salvation on the napkin, then looked up at Bob and said, "You've heard us talk a lot about Jesus this week. The fact is, I want you to know Jesus personally, so you can be saved and go to heaven. It is as easy as ABC: Ask, Believe, Confess."

I continued, "I want you to pray and think about this, and when you are ready, respond and ask Jesus to come into your life. Believe God raised Him from the dead, and confess He is Lord." To my surprise, Bob raised both hands and said, "I am ready now! I want to give my whole life to Jesus Christ!" It was a great morning of rejoicing for our team as Bob received Jesus into his life for the first time.

Many Hongs and Bobs are all around us, just waiting for someone to see them and share Jesus with them. It is easy—as easy as ABC!

But wait a moment! The story continues. While writing this book, I visited China once again. This time, I was invited by the government to visit registered churches and meet with three self-church leaders across one province. I was the first Western Christian leader officially invited into China since before the pandemic. A government agency even paid our expenses for the trip. We enjoyed a wonderful time connecting with our fellow believers, learning more about the present situation on the ground in China, and praying for leaders in every city.

The Chinese harvest continues to be ripe, and even with the restrictive environment through a global pandemic, God is moving significantly. Millions and millions of people know Jesus and millions more desperately need Him. As always, the spiritual hunger of the Chinese people was noticeable and significant. As I rode for hundreds of miles in a van or on a train, I saw thousands of high-rise condominiums and felt the enormity of our task again. How will we ever reach everyone in these vertical villages for Christ? Once again, the Holy Spirit reminded me: One person at a time!

During our visit, we were accompanied by a team of researchers and helpers. One young lady, whom I will call Sheila (real name withheld for protection), traveled with us on the team. Sheila was quiet and somewhat introverted, like a typical Generation Z twenty-seven-year-old. She was a college graduate and unassertively brilliant. Throughout the trip, our team conversed with everyone serving us, and we gave special attention to Sheila in an attempt to draw her into deeper conversation. Each time I spoke at a public gathering, she listened very intently from the edge of her seat, soaking in every word. She did not know much about Jesus but was open to learning more.

On the last day, as our core team stood in the train station preparing for the arduous trip home, I felt impressed to pray for her. I called Sheila aside and asked if she would allow me to pray for her. She agreed, and I prayed.

Sheila was genuinely grateful for my prayer and started to return to the group—however, I could not shake the sense that I needed to say something more to her, so I asked her to sit beside me for a moment. I then shared the ABCs of knowing Jesus. This time I didn't have a napkin, but Sheila's English was strong enough that she understood. After sharing for a few moments, I asked her if she believed, and she said, "Yes! I believe in Jesus." She told our team members through tears that she believed in Jesus and gave her heart to Christ right there in the train station.

Heaven rejoiced with us that day as another lost ONE was found. I cannot wait to hear all that Sheila will do for Christ in the days ahead as her potential to change the world is released.

WHOSOEVER BELIEVES

About twenty years after Martin Luther nailed his ninety-five theses to the door in Wittenberg, Germany, and the Protestant Reformation began, a man by the name of John Calvin began pastoring in the city of Geneva, Switzerland. Over approximately thirty years, he developed a thought process that became known as Calvinism. This Reformed tradition has both positive and negative points. In a discussion about the Great Commission, addressing these points has merit.

Admittedly, the next paragraphs will be a cursory, crash course in Calvin's teaching with a quick refutation of them. The shortness of this volume will not allow me to discuss this at length, but I believe that understanding some about this doctrine may help reclaim the urgency of the Great Commission that has been lost among many evangelical Christians.

Calvin was born in 1509, and while he was still young, his mother died. Calvin was raised by his father, who pushed him to become educated. Calvin was educated in Latin, Greek, and some Hebrew. Ultimately, he became a lawyer, but along the way, felt the impulse of God to follow Jesus Christ fully.[53]

By 1537, Calvin was pastoring in Geneva, which at the time was a crossroads that connected north and south, east and west. He sought to establish how protestants would be governed in society and, in many ways, sought to form a Christian utopia.

Along the way, he preached approximately 2,000 sermons and wrote his famous work, *Institutes of the Christian Religion.* This included eighty chapters filled with his teaching and understanding of God and the Scriptures. Calvin's teaching can be summarized in five points, each point beginning with an English letter that corresponds with a letter in the word, "TULIP."

The "T" represents "total depravity." Calvin believed that man was totally depraved, unable to save himself.

When Adam fell in the Garden of Eden, sin was cast on all human beings, and man became dead in sin. Only by grace could a person ever be saved.

The "U" in the TULIP acronym denotes "unconditional election." Calvin believed and taught that some people were predestined for heaven while others were predestined for hell. In *Institutes of the Christian Religion*, Calvin wrote, "All are not created on equal terms, but some are preordained to eternal life, others to eternal damnation; and, accordingly, as each has been created for one or other of these ends, we say that he has been predestinated to life or to death."[54] Calvin once claimed this was a horrific teaching, but he believed it nonetheless.

The "L," indicates "limited atonement." Calvin believed and taught that Jesus did not die for everyone's sins, but He died for the sins of the elect. In other words, he believed the atoning work of Jesus Christ on the cross was only for those predestined to be saved.

The "I" represents "irresistible grace." According to Calvin, man could not resist the grace of God, and once declared and predestined by God to be saved, grace commences to save and redeem a person without any input from the individual. Salvation is all a work of grace without any assent or response from the person. He taught that grace was irresistible, and that once destined to be saved, a person would be saved.

Finally, the "P" signifies the "perseverance of the saints." Calvin believed the redeemed would endure and ultimately be saved and that once a person was in grace, they would forever remain in grace. A person's eternal destiny was secured once they became a believer, and they would have no other choice.

This "TULIP" teaching—Total depravity, Unconditional election, Limited atonement, Irresistible grace, and Perseverance—became the bedrock of Calvin's teaching and continues to affect the Christian world even now, 500 years later.

Indeed, there are some positives in what John Calvin taught. He helped establish an understanding of the providence, control, and sovereignty of God. He also taught the separation of church and state and championed children's education. He sought to make Geneva a Protestant model of how a Christian community should look under this new philosophy that Christians are born again and changed by grace alone. These were significant contributions to society. Yet, there are many negatives to the doctrine of Calvinism that the church is still dealing with today.

First, the theology of Calvinism negates human free will. It also damages God's reputation as a good God and teaches He predestines people that He created for hell. Further, this Reformed tradition relegates only certain people to be saved, giving others no such chance. I believe that the teaching of Calvin undermines evangelistic fervor and cheapens the cross of Christ. It leaves the believer asking, "If God has already determined who will be saved, why preach the gospel?"

While in college, I had a friend and roommate, who believed in Calvinist teaching. His name was Kevin, and he came from a small Calvinistic denomination. While we were in school, Kevin sadly lost his mother to cancer. Because of what he had been taught, Kevin believed God had predetermined his mother would die from this disease. This was very depressing for Kevin, and one of his favorite sayings during the last two or three years of college was, "Life is a bummer." Whenever Kevin would say, "Life is a bummer," I would tell him, "Kevin, life is not a bummer. God is good." But he would say it repeatedly anyway.

I pastored people at times who believed in the "perseverance" part of Calvinism, and thus believed that no matter what they did with their life, they were still secure in Christ before God. This is simply not true, and it causes people to live without spiritual fervor or intensity. It is very hard to motivate them to draw close to Christ and walk full of the Holy Spirit. Why should they? They are already going to heaven.

When you believe sickness, suffering, and evil have been predestined by God, life indeed feels like a bummer. And when you do not believe in human free will, you have no motivation for Great Commission action. However, the truth is that God is good, and His heart is for everyone. I want to quickly address four points to counter Calvin's teachings.

First, God's sovereignty is absolute. The psalmist says, "For God is the King of all the Earth; sing to him a psalm of praise. God reigns over the nations; God is seated on his holy throne" (Psalm 47:7-8).

Second, God's foreknowledge is not pre-determinism, and His omniscience doesn't imply that He preordains everything. The Bible is filled with the word "if," seen first in the book of Genesis when God tells Cain, "If you do what is right, will you not be accepted? But if you do not do what is right, sin is crouching at your door; it desires to have you, but you must rule over it" (Genesis 4:7).

God's blessings in Scripture are portrayed repeatedly as contingent on man's response. Scripture says, "*If* my people, who are called by my name, will humble themselves and pray and seek my face and turn from their wicked ways, then I will hear from heaven, and I will forgive their sin and will heal their land" (2 Chronicles 7:14, emphasis added). This "if" is important. "If we will," God will hear from heaven. In His message to the Laodicean church, Jesus says, "Here I am! I stand at the door and knock. *If* anyone hears my voice and opens the door, I will come in and eat with that person, and they with me" (Revelation 3:20, emphasis added). Repeatedly in Scripture, we read the qualifier "if." If we respond correctly, we receive more of God's grace.

Third, while salvation comes solely through grace, you can resist it. Understanding the concept of free will is crucial in accepting that we are saved by God's grace alone and not by our efforts. Paul clarified for the Ephesian believers that our salvation is a gift from God, not a product of our works (see Ephesians 2:8–9). Grace is powerful. It pulls us out of our sinful state, transforms us, and empowers us to believe in Jesus Christ. His grace is available to everyone! We would do well to remind ourselves of Paul's words to Titus: "For the grace of God has appeared that offers salvation to *all people*" (2:1, emphasis added).

Fourth, Jesus died for everyone, not just for a select few. Jesus taught the religious Pharisee, Nicodemus, who questioned how one could be born again of the Spirit, "For God so loved the world, that he gave his only begotten Son, that *whosoever* believeth in him should not perish, but have everlasting life" (John 3:16, KJV, emphasis added).

Jesus died for everyone, not just for a select few.

Jesus died for everyone, and He desires everyone to know Him.

In many ways, Calvinism has been a detrimental force to God's kingdom, and at times, it has dulled the church's effectiveness. It is vitally important we understand God's Word as truth, so we can join Him in reaching everyone and fully accept His call to re-personalize the Great Commission. God invites one and all to be on mission with Christ, and God's grace is available to everyONE!

CHAPTER 5

THE WORLD IN WHICH EVERYONE MUST BE REACHED

The 21st century will be the most volatile in history. If we are going to reach everyone on Earth with the gospel of Jesus Christ, we will do so amid the drama and trauma of this age.

EVERYONE WHO CALLS ON THE NAME

Peter stood trembling under the power of God. They were celebrating Pentecost and experiencing Jesus' promise that they would receive power. The long wait had ended, and the Comforter had come. Wind, fire, tongues, and spiritual authority exploded into the Earth. The early church was born and empowered by the Holy Spirit at the same time. The glory of God filled the followers of Jesus, and the

Spirit who had been with them was now living in them. A new day was dawning.

People from nations around the world were in Jerusalem for the feast of Pentecost and heard the wonders of God in their own tongue as the Holy Spirit demonstrated His missionary intent. Never in history had this phenomenon been witnessed. Many were amazed, while others were confused. Clarity was needed. Peter stood up and raised his voice to explain.

He noted that the people were not drunk with natural wine since it was early in the morning, and what was being experienced was in direct fulfillment of God's Word through Joel:

"And afterward, I will pour out my Spirit on all people. Your sons and daughters will prophesy, your old men will dream dreams, your young men will see visions. Even on my servants, both men and women, I will pour out my Spirit in those days. I will show wonders in the heavens and on the earth, blood and fire and billows of smoke. The sun will be turned to darkness and the moon to blood before the coming of the great and dreadful day of the LORD. And everyone who calls on the name of the LORD will be saved" (Joel 2:28–32).

Joel's proclamation of God's promise was being fulfilled, and this meant all people everywhere would be touched by the Holy Spirit. The outpouring would be global and intergenerational, with young and old receiving supernatural insight. Both men and women would be blessed and used by God.

Peter declared clearly that the promise spoken of through the prophet Joel is what believers were experiencing on the day of Pentecost. He continued reciting Joel's prophecy that when the Spirit is poured out on all flesh, God would grant wonders and strange happenings, in both the heavens and the Earth. And, amid this drama and trauma, "EveryONE who calls on the name of the Lord will be saved" (Acts 2:21, emphasis added).

That very day in Jerusalem, more than 3,000 people would call on the name of the Lord and be redeemed.

According to Matthew's gospel, Jesus had also predicted days of extreme volatility at the end of the age. He spoke of an environment of deception, war, rumors of war, nation rising against nation, and kingdom rising against kingdom. He warned there would be natural disasters and intense persecution, and many who were once faithful would fall away from the faith. Yet, Jesus promised, "And this gospel of the kingdom will be preached in the whole world as a testimony to all nations, and then the end will come" (Matthew 24:14).

Amid the distressing bad news, God's good news would be preached.

These passages and many others help us understand that the environment in which every person on Earth will be reached with the gospel of Jesus will be difficult and unstable. This instability will serve to open the hearts of people to the message of Jesus, who is the same yesterday, today, and forever.

UNSTABLE TIMES

The environment described in Joel Chapter 2 and Matthew Chapter 24 is now our 21st-century reality. Chaos surrounds us. Wars are raging in Ukraine, Afghanistan, and parts of Africa; Christian brothers and sisters around the world are facing intense and growing persecution; gun violence is at an all-time high in the West; natural disasters are increasing in frequency and intensity; corrupt politics are damaging nations; and ungodly agendas tear at the family unit. In an age of mass media, polarizing outlooks, discord, and misinformation, deceit runs rampant. Truth and morality have become relative, and many—even within the church—have been swept away by false doctrine and the empty promises of deconstructionism.

During the last century, our world has undergone a series of breathtaking transformations, changing and shifting at a pace unmatched by nearly all the preceding history of humankind.

In 1900, the average life expectancy was less than forty-seven years of age.[55] It is now more than seventy-two.[56]

Before 1906, the year the Azusa Street revival began, people were still riding horses as their principal mode of transportation.

During the 20th century, scientific and technological discoveries exploded.

In 1903, the Wright brothers flew their first airplane at Kitty Hawk, North Carolina.[57] Now, approximately 100,000 commercial flights take place daily around the world, with more than 6,000,000 people flying somewhere each day.[58]

In 1927, the first television was demonstrated.[59] Now more than eighty percent of the world's households have at least one TV.

In 1969, a man took his first steps on the moon.[60]

In 1973, the first Global Positioning Device (GPS) was invented. Now more than ninety-three percent of drivers in the United States depend on it.[61]

In 1983, the internet was invented, and in 2023, it has more than five billion users worldwide.[62]

In 1994, the retail giant Amazon was founded, changing the way people shop forever.[63]

In 1996, scientists at Scotland's Roslin Institute became the first to clone a mammal, successfully cloning Dolly the sheep.[64]

In 1997, the first recognizable social media platform, Six Degrees, was founded and paved the way for today's social media eruption.[65]

In 1998, Google was founded. This search engine is now visited more than eighty-nine billion times a month.[66]

In 2004, Facebook was founded. In 2017, Facebook stats revealed two billion global users for the first time.[67]

In 2007, Apple unveiled the iPhone, a device that would irrevocably transform the world. There are presently over 1.5 billion iPhone users in the world.[68]

In 2021, the parent company of Facebook rebranded to "Meta," reinforcing the rise of the "metaverse," a fully immersive, augmented, and virtual reality experience.[69]

On November 30, 2022, the company OpenAI released the world's first fully interactive artificial intelligent chatbot, Chat GPT, with the ability to produce incredibly human-like responses and a tremendous wealth of knowledge in nearly every field of study. On May 16, 2023, the creator of

Chat GPT and CEO of OpenAI, Sam Altman, testified before the United States Congress that the technology was too powerful and could do significant harm to the world.[70]

During this century, the knowledge base of the world has multiplied exponentially.

In 1900, it took approximately 100 years to double the knowledge of the world.

By the mid-20th century, it took twenty-five years for knowledge to double.

A few years ago, it took fewer than twelve months.

Now the world's knowledge doubles every twelve hours.[71]

In 1928, the world population had just topped two billion. Today, across 195 million square miles, seven continents, 195 countries, and more than 10,000 cities, the staggering global population of eight billion continues to rise by greater than 200,000 people each day.

We are in unprecedented times in which society is evolving at lightning speed. With and beyond these changes, in the 21st century, basic understandings of truth, respect for life, acceptance of God's order, and general knowledge of right and wrong enforced by a unified legal code have all eroded into moral relativism and the removal of absolutes. All of these forces have worked together to destroy the foundational understandings of society and even the church. Judeo-Christian morality based on Scripture has deteriorated or been cast away by many in the West.

Moral relativism says there is no absolute truth or right and wrong, and many have fallen prey to the belief they can define their reality. With eight billion people on the planet, one might say we have eight billion versions of "truth" in the world, which has brought about great spiritual instability.

COLLAPSING FOUNDATIONS AND SIGNIFICANT SHAKING

"When the foundations are being destroyed, what can the righteous do?" (Psalm 11:3).

As foundations are being destroyed, eroded, and deteriorated, a significant spiritual shaking is also taking place. In many ways, these forces are forming a perfect spiritual storm. The seismic shifts in our world feel monumental.

What is happening spiritually was tragically demonstrated recently by the physical effect of the February 2023 earthquake in both Turkey and Syria, in which 3,000 buildings collapsed. Because of dated structures, new construction codes not followed, and shortcuts taken, the buildings could not endure the shaking of two back-to-back 7.0 earthquakes. Buildings with eroded foundations or compromised construction processes were doomed to collapse. In contrast, those buildings that were structurally sound remained standing.

While foundations are eroding and being destroyed, we are also witnessing a shaking throughout the kingdom of God that is revealing faulty construction and uncertain foundations. The writer of Hebrews warns us:

"His voice that time shook the earth to its foundations; this time—he's told us this quite plainly—he'll also rock the heavens: 'One last shaking, from top to bottom, stem to stern.' The phrase 'one last shaking' means a thorough housecleaning, getting rid of all the historical and religious junk so that the unshakable essentials stand clear and uncluttered" (Hebrews 12:26–27, MSG).

> **He has promised to shake down lies and deceptions so that what remains will be foundational and true.**

Some of the uncertainty of our time and the "shaking" we sense occurring is God at work. He has promised to shake down lies and deceptions so that what remains will be foundational and true. Ultimately, only those lives built on Jesus Christ—the everlasting rock—will endure.

CALLED AMID CRISIS

When Isaiah received his call to ministry, as recorded in Isaiah Chapter 6, the nation of Judah was facing a profound leadership crisis compounded by moral deterioration. The nation was being shaken dramatically.

Uzziah became king of Judah when he was sixteen years old and was in leadership for fifty-two years. King Uzziah was the only king Isaiah had known and was one of the most prosperous kings in Judah's history. "He sought God during the days of Zechariah, who instructed him in the fear of God. As long as he sought the LORD, God gave him success" (2 Chronicles 26:5).

Uzziah's rule started strong, and as he acknowledged the Lord, he was given great success by God. During his reign, Judah consistently conquered their enemies, including the Philistines. They had a 3,000-man standing army, the economy was stable and prosperous, and King Uzziah was popular among the people of Judah and around the world. He was an influencer, and his kingdom was filled with innovation. Uzziah was a great leader . . . until he wasn't.

What eventually happened to this once-powerful king? "But after Uzziah became powerful, his pride led to his downfall. He was unfaithful to the LORD his God" (2 Chronicles 26:16).

King Uzziah was perhaps the most powerful and successful person in the world, but as such, he allowed pride to enter his heart. He soon forgot that it was God who elevated him to this position and blessed his kingdom. His pride led to disobedience, and ultimately, his death. He reigned as king for more than half a century, yet died as a leper and a pauper. His death shook Judah to its foundational core.

The 21st century has been marked by a wave of leadership failures in nearly every sphere of society around the globe. From Australia to Africa, from the USA to Europe, from the political corridors of Capitol Hill to the tech hubs of Silicon Valley, leaders have lost their way morally, relationally, financially, and in terms of their integrity. This global failure of leadership has not spared any institution, including the church. The millennial church, in particular, is undergoing a revolutionary correction as a long-standing culture of performance and popularity devoid of depth and authenticity is being judged and torn down.

Godly leaders should be encouraged in these times by these words: "A thousand may fall at your side, ten thousand at your right hand, but it will not come near you" (Psalms 91:7).

While Judah reeled from the loss of its beloved king, Isaiah looked for stability in God, his rock. The prophet's transformational search begins with these words: "In the year that King Uzziah died, I saw the Lord, high and exalted, seated on a throne; and the train of his robe filled the temple" (Isaiah 6:1).

While the foundations of Judah's kingdom seemed to collapse, Isaiah saw that their true foundation, the living God, was still on the throne. God was not shaken.

DYNAMIC STABILITY

In 2022, a survey was taken by Handshake, an employment site for Generation Z. The surveyors asked 1,800 new graduates what they most wanted from their future employers. The overwhelming majority (eighty-five percent) answered "stability." The desire for a fast-growing company, however, garnered only twenty-nine percent of the vote.[72]

Generation Z and our entire world long for stability. Some have said it is one of the six greatest human needs. So, in a world of instability, how do we find it? If we are going to reach everyone on the planet, I believe we need dynamic stability to help us stay strong and keep moving forward lest we fall short of the call of God.

In engineering, "dynamic stability" refers to the ability of an airplane to return to a stable flight after encountering turbulence. While the plane is moving forward, the tilt of the wings allows the airplane to remain above the Earth and overcome the forces of gravity. After experiencing turbulence, the airplane must keep moving forward aggressively to regain stability. It is this dynamic stability that allows you to sit on a plane moving at a speed of more than 500 miles per hour yet feel as if you are sitting perfectly still. Similarly, dynamic stability in the context of our spiritual lives refers to our ability to remain steadfast in our faith and our walk with God even as we navigate the turbulence of our times.

We need dynamic stability to help us stay strong and keep moving forward lest we fall short of the call of God.

Dynamic stability is only made possible by the act of continual motion. Gale force winds are pressing in around us—winds of doctrine, change, and adversity. Many lives are not able to withstand these forces. Although the storms may howl around us and society may feel more unstable than ever, we can continue to advance undeterred when we maintain forward spiritual movement. We can find stability in the face of shaking foundations, seismic shifts, and battering winds. Turbulence need not destroy us. It may cause us to oscillate, but if we follow God and move forward with Him, we will return to dynamic stability.

How exactly do we develop this dynamic stability in our lives to continue moving forward and pursuing the lost?

With all that is occurring in our world, we may face the temptation to sit very still in an attempt to remain stable, but if we choose to hide away, we will be destroyed.

The only way to acquire stability is to first stand in awe of the living God. To maintain stability in turbulence, we keep aggressively moving forward and trusting God fully.

The Christian life should be one of dynamic stability, or as some might explain it, active rest. Paul tells the Corinthians, "Be ye steadfast, unmovable, always abounding in the work of the Lord" (1 Corinthians 15:58, KJV). He is telling them to be stable, but not still, always on the move.

The psalmist declared, "I've been slandered unmercifully by the politicians, but my awe at your words keeps me stable" (Psalm 119:161, MSG).

The prophet Isaiah encourages us to understand, "God keeps your days stable and secure—salvation, wisdom, and knowledge in surplus, and best of all, Zion's treasure, Fear-of-God" (Isaiah 33:6, MSG).

The writer of Hebrews skillfully employs a question-and-answer motif to encourage and challenge us: "Do you see what we've got? An unshakable kingdom! And do you see how thankful we must be? Not only thankful but brimming with worship, deeply reverent before God. For God is not an indifferent bystander. He's actively cleaning the house, torching all that needs to burn, and he won't quit until it's all cleansed. God himself is Fire!" (Hebrews 12:28–29, MSG).

Indisputably, we serve a God who is stable. He is the same yesterday, today, and forever; He is our rock and fortress; He is a mighty and dependable God; He never sleeps nor slumbers; He will always be there, and we can rest secure in Him. At the same time, God is dynamic and always on the move. He is dynamically stable.

In contrast, the people in Old Testament times would create idols that appeared stable, but they were not. Instead, these idols were dead. They had eyes, but they couldn't see; they had ears, but they couldn't hear; they had mouths, but they couldn't speak. They were made in man's image, hoping they would be dependable and unchanging, but they did not deliver.

We would do well to remind ourselves that Jehovah God is a living God. He is both a rock and a consuming fire. "The earth is the LORD's, and everything in it, the world, and all who live in it" (Psalm 24:1). Therefore, those of us who are a part of His kingdom can and should live a dynamic life while also living with great stability—even in unstable cultural and economic times.

Essentially, if we are going to live with stability, we must keep pouring out. An airplane will crash if it quits moving, and even so, Christians will crash when they stop serving and witnessing. As a believer, you must stay on the move with God.

Jeremiah, the prophet, speaks about the nation of Moab and the people's spiritual laziness. He prophesied that God was about to judge them for their complacency. "Moab has been at rest from youth, like wine left on its dregs, not poured from one jar to another—she has not gone into exile. So, she tastes as she did, and her aroma is unchanged" (48:11). Because Moab had not been pouring out, she was facing judgment. God used the illustration of wine left on its dregs to explain what this had done to them as a people.

When it is first made, wine has dregs—or "impurities"— that settle to the bottom of the vessel. One of the ways to rid the wine of its impurities is to pour it from one vessel to another. This refines the wine, allowing it to breathe, and leaves the old, bitter dregs behind. In the same way, when we refuse to be poured from one situation to another, and we refuse to follow God—moving from glory to glory—we "settle on the dregs." When we are not being poured out into the lives of others, we will become sour, bitter, and impure. We must keep moving with God and be willing to be poured out, bringing refreshing ministry to others. This pouring process refines and purifies us, preventing us from becoming stale.

Another great illustration of this concept is the Dead Sea. The Dead Sea is the lowest place on Earth and has no outlet. Sixty-five miles north of the Dead Sea is the Sea of Galilee, and flowing down from it is the Jordan River, which takes the water from the Sea of Galilee and brings it into the Dead Sea.

Unlike the Dead Sea, the Sea of Galilee and the Jordan River are full of resources for the Holy Land. But after flowing downward for sixty-five miles, the beautiful, life-giving waters of the Jordan become the bitter, lifeless water of the Dead Sea. The Dead Sea is unable to sustain life because it has no outlet, and as a result, the water stops moving and flowing. It is a collecting point, always receiving but never giving.

Similarly, as a believer, if you are always receiving but never giving, you will die spiritually.

We must continue moving with God, following His lead, and pouring into the people around us. Witnessing to the lost is a dynamic and purifying activity in our lives. It is essential if we are going to stay right before God and remain steadfast in a world of instability.

The world needs people who are stable and moving with God amid the turbulence.

The world needs people who are stable and moving with God amid the turbulence. They need to see a faith that isn't shaken, and they need to hear the good news of Jesus Christ. Participating in the mission to reach everyone on Earth for Christ will position us to live lives of dynamic stability.

CALLING REQUIRES CLEANSING

Isaiah was called amidst a leadership crisis and also faced a moral crisis in Judah. The people were struggling spiritually. God's law was neglected, injustice was rampant, oppression was normalized, prayer was peripheral, and idolatry and immorality were prevalent. Judah's sin would be its downfall. Isaiah was called to speak on God's behalf in an environment in which the moral framework of the nation was collapsing all around him.

The biblical principle is clear: "Righteousness exalts a nation, but sin condemns any people" (Proverbs 14:34).

Like Isaiah's world, the world in which we live and lead is in steep moral decline. Societies across the globe have embraced perversion, pornography, and pride, instead of embracing God's righteousness. We are living in a morally confused and spiritually depressed world.

Isaiah's encounter with a Holy God in an unholy world would set him apart and allow him to minister while maintaining his spiritual integrity. "Woe to me," Isaiah would cry at the sight of God's holiness in heaven. "I am ruined! For I am a man of unclean lips, and I live among a people of unclean lips" (6:5). Isaiah would then experience supernatural cleansing as one of the seraphim (a burner angel) took a live coal from the altar of heaven and purged his lips on Earth. This cleansing was critical if Isaiah was going to be effective in delivering God's message to his generation.

I am convinced that today's church and many of today's believers will not be effective in winning others for Christ or reaching individuals around us until we experience supernatural cleansing. Our desire to reach broken and spiritually bruised people will ultimately drive us to experience spiritual cleansing so we can be effective.

Not long after David committed adultery with Bathsheba and became the instigator of her husband Uriah's death, he was confronted by the prophet Nathan.

Nathan fearlessly helped David see himself before God, and David repented (2 Samuel 11–12). During his prayer of repentance, David cried out for mercy and cleansing. He grieved deeply for his sins and longed for God's presence to remain with him. In his brokenness, David prayed: "Restore to me the joy of your salvation and grant me a willing spirit, to sustain me. **Then I will teach transgressors your ways so that sinners will turn back to you**" (Psalms 51:12–13, emphasis added).

David's experience of cleansing would lead to effectiveness in reaching transgressors and sinners. Likewise, the 21st century church needs a deep purging: a fire from the altar, a prophetic confrontation, and a season of extreme humility that will lead to cleansing, restoration, and effectiveness in reaching the lost. Isaiah's encounter with God's fire speaks to us now as we live in this world of moral decay.

RESISTANCE EXPECTED

In addition to facing corporate shaking and foundational deterioration, Isaiah would also encounter significant resistance. After accepting God's call, Isaiah was told by the Lord, "I want you to go preach to these people, but they will not listen to you. The more you preach to them, the harder their hearts will become" (Isaiah 6:9, paraphrased). The drama and trauma in Judah during Isaiah's ministry meant that his message would not always be accepted. He would encounter consistent resistance.

As we enter this new era of evangelism, focused on reaching everyone on Earth, we must be prepared for significant spiritual warfare. The eternal stakes are high, so the battle is going to be severe.

This battle ahead will transcend the brazen actions of individuals. Paul instructs us, "Our struggle is not against flesh and blood" (Ephesians 6:12). We wage war in the spiritual, and invisible (and visible) resistance is inevitable when doing the will of God.

> **This battle ahead will transcend the brazen actions of individuals.**

THE GARDEN PRINCIPLE

In the Garden of Eden, God reveals a formula for the spiritual warfare that will take place on Earth as His kingdom and plan of redemption are advanced. I have found that this principle—or "equation"—has been true multiple times in my ministry: If you are going to hurt Satan's kingdom, you should expect to get bruised and wounded in the process. The volatility and moral decline of our day make this truer than ever.

When God confronts Adam and Eve following their disobedience in the garden, He states the consequences or curses brought about by their actions. God also curses the serpent and, representatively, Satan and his minions: "I'm declaring war between you and the woman, between your offspring and hers. He'll wound your head, you'll wound (bruise) his heel" (Genesis 3:15, MSG).

This principle of spiritual warfare has endured. We crush Satan's head and overthrow his kingdom, but in the process, our heel is bruised or wounded. Many times, the greater the victory, the greater the wounding or bruising.

Many years ago, I traveled to Rajahmundry, India, to conduct a youth camp for young people in a compound that was led by our denominational leader in India. During those years, our ministry involved traveling to different nations, establishing youth camp ministries, and teaching indigenous leaders how to direct an effective camping ministry.

Getting to Rajahmundry in those days was difficult and exhausting, to say the least. Hours on an airplane were followed by more than twenty hours on an ancient-feeling train, followed by several hours in a car or van. Finally, we arrived and began welcoming young people to the youth camp.

Camping ministry has always been one of my favorite ministry activities. Something happens when young people pull away and focus on God in a compact, intense way that is difficult to explain. Once you experience and see the lives that are changed in camp, you will be a fan of this ministry method. I certainly am.

While in India, we were excited to teach camping ministry to our hosts while doing a model camp with them. Our team was thrilled to be in Rajahmundry though we were eating a variety of very unusual things!

We brought games from America, including softball bats and balls to teach American baseball to the campers. We were fairly ignorant that India is one of the great nations in the world for cricket, so they don't play baseball too often. Nonetheless, we intended to have fun and see God touch the lives of young people. Days at the camp were filled with activity, learning, devotions, fun times, and evening services where I would preach, and we would invite the students to either receive Jesus or experience more of Him.

On the third night of these powerful evening services, I preached a message that was focused on the cross. Though the camp was held more than thirty years ago, I can still remember the message I preached. I used a wooden cross as a prop and talked about the magnetic power of Jesus' love when it was demonstrated through His death on the cross.

When I gave the invitation that evening, something strange happened. An older man, who had been sitting outside the chapel building on the wall of the compound listening to the services for a couple of nights (Americans in Rajahmundry in those days were a public spectacle), came into the chapel and walked all the way to the front. He knelt at the altar and, after a few moments, surrendered his life to Christ. He would testify that he now believed in Jesus as his Savior and was going to serve the Lord.

The Indian leaders present became very excited about his conversion. They explained to me that evening that this older gentleman had been a Hindu his entire life and that he was one of the meanest men in town. He was a person who rejected and fought against Christianity and was one of the enemies of the progress of their work. They were surprised and thrilled that this man surrendered his life to Jesus and believed the message of the cross. It was like Saul of Tarsus being saved all over again.

That night, I crawled into my bed in the compound, rejoicing about the Lord's blessing. The plane ride, the train ride, the rough roads, the hard work of the trip, and even the exotic food all seemed worth it to see these young

Indian people touched by God. I was especially thrilled to witness this Hindu man at the end of his life find Jesus as his Savior. Satan's kingdom had been damaged in Rajahmundry.

I slept well until the early morning when suddenly I felt something grab one of my fingers. This hurt enough to startle and awaken me. As I rose from the bed, I saw a rat about the size of a small rabbit scamper down my body, off the bed, and out the door. Without thinking, I shouted, "I rebuke you, devil!" Then, I realized my finger had been bitten by the rat. Gratefully, the skin wasn't broken, but the adrenaline rush of the moment is something I will never forget.

Later that day, our team's softball bats became very useful as the same rat (at least we think it was the same one) scrambled into one of the ladies' suitcases. Screams ensued, and the men on the team ran upstairs to her room to see if they could help. For a while, they could not find the rat, but then one of the team saw a rat's tail sticking out from under a piece of furniture. He stepped on the tail and moved the furniture while another team member hit a home run with the rat. It was a successful team effort.

Even now, I am convinced that the rat bite was one small way the enemy was retaliating against me for the

Hindu man being saved. In India and Hinduism, animals are revered, and things like bulls, monkeys, and yes, even rats are worshiped. Hindu belief is that all life should be honored and never harmed. This includes rats. There is even a temple in India, the Karni Mata Temple of Deshnok, that is dedicated to rats.

When the rat bit me, I immediately associated the affront with the enemy fighting against the gospel and wounding my hand (instead of my heel). Paul was bitten by a snake on Malta, so I guess being bitten by a rat in India was suitable for gospel work.

If we are going to rescue the lost and help them escape from the kingdom of darkness, we should expect resistance.

The principle remains the same. If we are going to rescue the lost and help them escape from the kingdom of darkness, we should expect resistance and retaliation from the darkness. If we bruise the enemy's kingdom, we will be bruised. Isaiah's bruising and wounding would come in the form of rejection from those he loved and prophesied to.

SEND ME ANYWAY!

Isaiah faced a societal upheaval, a leadership crisis, moral deterioration, and significant resistance from the kingdom of darkness. Yet, as he encountered God's presence and experienced supernatural cleansing, he was prepared to hear God's voice. He then heard the voice of his Master, Jehovah, saying: "Whom shall I send? Who will go for us?" (6:8). **Isaiah spoke up. "I'll go. Send me!"**

Isaiah volunteered for the difficult task of carrying God's news to His people. He did not shrink back or allow fear to restrain him. He boldly accepted the challenge and, amid the drama and trauma of his day, became a bearer of good news. Isaiah overcame his weaknesses and ministered in God's strength.

People throughout Scripture were called despite their weaknesses and struggles. Abraham was too old; Jeremiah was too young; Elijah was suicidal; Joseph had been abused; Job went bankrupt; Moses stuttered; Gideon had low self-esteem; Samson had a problem with women; Rahab was a prostitute; Hosea had an immoral wife; Peter lacked moral courage under pressure; and Paul persecuted the church and lived with a thorn in the flesh. All were imperfect people whom God used despite their weaknesses as they responded, "Here am I, use me anyway!"

God specializes in using imperfect people. This is good news and means He can use you and me if we will answer His call.

Despite the tremors of leadership failure, foundational moral deterioration, significant resistance, and even our weaknesses, may we humbly answer His call, "Here am I, Lord, send me anyway! Send me to a world full of individuals needing to hear the good news of Jesus Christ."

God specializes in using imperfect people. This is good news and means He can use you and me if we will answer His call.

Throughout history, we find amazing examples of people who faced trials and turbulence but were willing to endure hardship to do God's will. William Carey, the father of modern-day missions,[73] is one such example.

As a young man in England, Carey started his career as a shoe cobbler. But soon, he was gripped by the need for the gospel to go to the unreached. In his shop, Carey took a piece of cowhide and carved a map of the world in it. Every day, he would look at the map and pray until finally, he became an answer to his own prayers: He decided to leave his career behind and take his family to India.

At this time, India was unevangelized, and the journey there was very time-consuming and arduous (even worse than my journey to Rajahmundry). Carey and his family made the trek but faced extreme difficulty. Within a few years, Carey's ministry partner quit and returned to England. Carey's five-year-old son died of dysentery, and his wife became severely mentally ill. At one point, he experienced a fire, and all he had built burned to the ground.

He faced hardship after hardship, and seven years of hard work in India were required before Carey baptized his first convert. And after forty-one years of serving without a furlough, Carey had only gained 700 converts.

Additionally, Carey translated the Bible into all of India's major languages and portions of the Scripture into more than 100 dialects. His missional theme was, "Expect great things from God, attempt great things for God." Through all the adversity and hard work, Carey paved the way for modern-day missions and Christian witness in India.

Today, there are millions of believers in India because
of the work of William Carey and those few who followed
him. Despite the difficulty, turbulence, and hardship, Carey
had a burden for lost souls. He followed the call of God
and made a tremendous impact on the world. Whatever
it costs, may the cry of this generation be, "Lord, send
me anyway!"

NO MORE OF THIS!

In these times of drama, trauma, and instability, believers
have wrestled with how to correctly respond to the spiritual
and moral decay being witnessed in our world. For some,
the answer has been through dramatic political action. The
convergence of faith and government has been a hot topic
in recent years and one that needs to be firmly addressed as
we work to fulfill the Great Commission.

Let's start by going back to the night before
Jesus' crucifixion.

In an olive grove east of Jerusalem, known as the Garden
of Gethsemane, Jesus retreated in the night to pray. He
had already dined with His disciples and was fully aware
of what was ahead. The next day would be the crucifixion,
the apex of His coming to Earth. With anticipation, He

felt the weight of what He would soon endure. In intense anguish, Jesus began sweating drops of blood as He prayed, "Father if you are willing, take this cup from me." He was aware of the suffering to come, and His flesh was aching to be spared. But Jesus continued, "Yet not my will Lord, but yours be done" (Luke 22:42). He knew what He must do to accomplish God's will and save the world.

Some of Jesus' disciples were with Him in the garden, but when He rose from prayer and walked back to where they were, He found Peter, James, and John fast asleep. Disappointed, He asked, "Why are you sleeping? Couldn't you keep watch for just one hour? The time has come. Get up."

As they looked into the distance, a group of soldiers and Pharisees drew near, and unexpectedly, Judas approached Jesus. With a kiss, he signaled to nearby soldiers who Jesus was, and they were ready to make the arrest. "Judas, why are you betraying the Son of Man with a kiss?" Jesus asked (v. 28).

As the soldiers drew their weapons and chains making their way toward Jesus, the disciples became anxious. Peter quickly drew his sword, and in an impulsive instant, cut off the ear of Malchus, the high priest's servant. Overzealous, Peter was ready to fight, thinking it was the right thing to do.

At that moment, Jesus didn't thank Peter or draw His sword. He also did not encourage the disciples to charge against the soldier or initiate a rebellion. Instead, He rebuked Peter saying, "No more of this!" Jesus then leaned down and picked up Malchus' ear from the Gethsemane dirt. He gently placed the ear back on Malchus' head, healing him and restoring his ability to hear (vv. 49–51).

By drawing his sword with zeal to fight, Peter chose to use Roman ways instead of God's way. Peter caused this man, who would later be standing at the trial of Jesus hearing his testimony to experience auditory incapacitation. Peter decided to act like the world instead of acting like Jesus.

Like Peter, the church, in parts of the world today, has abandoned God's way and traded them for the world's methods. In turbulent and unstable times, the incorrect route has often been taken in wielding a political sword and seeking to use force to move God's kingdom agenda forward. Of course, this has not worked and never will. In using worldly methods while seeking heavenly results, we may have incapacitated the hearing of this generation toward the gospel.

I believe that, in the United States in particular, an entire generation's hearing has been damaged because the church has tried to use the ways of the world to change the world. At times, these actions have been so loud that they have muffled or suppressed God's voice. We are experiencing an auditory eclipse where Christians are standing in the way of unbelievers hearing the voice of Jesus and His invitation to know God. Because of our actions, the world has stopped listening to the gospel.

Jesus said to Peter and His apostles, "No more of this!" I hear the same in my spirit that the Lord of Heaven and Earth is making this declaration to us today. We must stop the madness and regain the hearing of a generation that has been deafened by the world's ideologies both inside and outside the church. The survival and success of the church—particularly the Western Church—rely on

We must stop the madness and regain the hearing of a generation that has been deafened by the world's ideologies both inside and outside the church.

us refocusing our attention on the main thing: A generation that needs to know the Jesus who can redeem their life.

I've contended for many years that the way a nation is changed is not in the White House or Congressional House, but in the church house and our own houses. Nations are changed from the bottom up, rather than the top down. The assumption that "If we only have the right person in power, righteousness will be established in our nation," is a misnomer.

Yes, we should vote, and yes, we should seek positive change in political systems, but we must not be inebriated by the elixir of political power, presuming that we are pleasing God in the process. Jesus' kingdom is not of this world, but it is powerful and world-changing. This change will only happen from the ground up, one heart at a time.

In following Jesus' declaration at Gethsemane, "No more of this," the early church refused to use force or worldly ways in seeking to change the world. For the first three hundred years of Christianity, swords and weapons were not used to advance Christianity. Instead, the early church used the greater weapons of love, prayer, spiritual fruit, supernatural gifts, and personal witness to turn the world upside down. Rome was changed from the inside out, not from the top down.

A. J. Gordon said, "Ecclesiastical corpses lie all about us. The caskets in which they repose are lined with satin and decorated with flowers. Like the other caskets, they are just large enough for their own occupants with no room for converts. These churches have died of respectability and have been embalmed in self-complacency. If, by the grace of God, our church (movement) is alive, be warned of our opportunity, or the feet of them that buried thy sisters will be at the door to carry thee out."[74]

Let us wean ourselves off the poison of Earthly power. No more of this! Instead, let us focus on healing the wounded ears of this generation so that they can hear the voice of the living God inviting them into His kingdom.

A BOLD CHURCH IN A FEARFUL WORLD

While we are called to lay down the world's methods and focus on being more like Jesus, this does not mean we are to yield to timidity. Jesus was humble, gentle, and kind, but He was also bold, committed, and strong. In a chaotic world, the church needs boldness to face the tide against us and continue pressing forward.

In Acts Chapters 1 and 2, Luke shares an account of the days following Jesus' ascension to heaven and the birth of the church. The disciples, once afraid and scattered after Jesus' crucifixion, were huddled together praying in the upper room in Jerusalem. The world outside their door was a storm of hostility and uncertainty. Jerusalem's streets had just been blood-stained with the execution of Jesus and now echoed with rumors of a Jewish uprising evoking Roman retaliation. Yet amid this turbulent backdrop, these ordinary men and women waited with anticipation for the fulfillment of Jesus' promise: "Do not leave Jerusalem but wait for the gift my Father promised, which you have heard me speak about. For John baptized with water, but in a few days you will be baptized with the Holy Spirit" (Acts 1:4–5).

As they waited, they cried out in prayer for strength to face the future. The world was a dangerous, volatile place, and they would need spiritual power to fulfill Jesus' command to reach the nations. The promise of Jesus would be realized, and when the Holy Spirit came on them, they would become witnesses to the ends of the Earth. The Holy Spirit transformed these ordinary men and women into bold witnesses. They were empowered by the Spirit to reach and change the world.

Fast forward approximately 2,000 years, and here we are today with new trauma and drama surrounding us. The heavens and the Earth are destabilized with spiritual shaking. The velocity and moral emptiness of our age has prepared the hearts of billions for the good news we are called to share. Everyone needs this message. Yet . . .

One preacher can't reach everyone.

One influencer can't reach everyone.

One institution can't reach everyone.

One denomination or movement can't reach everyone.

No one group, movement, person, technology, or initiative can reach everyone.

Reaching everyONE will require everyone.

CHAPTER 6

A NEW ERA OF EVANGELISM

Sunday, December 7, 1941, is a day that will live in infamy. In an early morning surprise raid, Japanese warplanes and submarines launched an attack on Pearl Harbor in Hawaii.[75] For one hour and fifteen minutes, bombs and bullets flew ending in nineteen U.S. warships and more than 400 U.S. aircraft lost or damaged. More than 2,400 U.S. Armed Forces personnel were killed, and 1,100 were wounded during the raid.

Several years ago, I had the privilege to visit a monument to one of those sunken ships, the USS Arizona, and her 1,177 dead crewmen, who are still resting at the bottom of Pearl Harbor. Deep sadness and soberness bathe the monument in a continuation of the profound loss experienced that day. The raid by the Japanese was one of the most successful surprise raids of all time. National shock quickly turned to national anger and mobilized the United States to officially enter World War II the following day.

President Franklin D. Roosevelt[76] wanted to immediately strike back against the Japanese for both strategic and national morale reasons. He felt that the citizens of the United States needed a rallying point, and Japan needed to know America would fight back. Roosevelt pushed for an attack on Tokyo, the heart of the Japanese empire. His request for an airstrike on Tokyo was a difficult one since many of the U.S. Navy's carriers and warships had either been sunk or severely damaged at Pearl Harbor, and American forces were not yet well-equipped to face the formidable defenses surrounding the island of Japan. But despite numerous obstacles, Roosevelt persisted, and a daring plan entitled the Doolittle Raid was devised.[77]

The raid was named after Lieutenant Colonel James Doolittle, who planned and led the attack. The Doolittle raid would involve sixteen B-25 bombers carried by the USS Hornet—an 873-foot-long aircraft carrier. The Hornet would travel within striking range of Tokyo and launch the sixteen bombers manned by volunteers from the Seventeenth Air Force bombardment group. The plan was to fly over Tokyo, execute the attack, and then continue to a landing in China.

On April 18, 1942, the planes were launched from the Hornet earlier than expected due to being spotted by a Japanese patrol boat. Despite a much longer distance to fly, the mission was accomplished, and select targets were bombed in Tokyo. As the planes continued in flight into the darkness over China, most of the crews suffered crash landings, and all but one of the aircraft in the raid were lost. Three men died in the aftermath of the raid and eight were captured by the Japanese. Of those who were captured, one died of starvation, three were shot by firing squads, and four survived in Japanese prisoner-of-war camps.

Among the prisoners was Jacob DeShazer,[78] whose crew bombed the city of Nagoya during the raid. He was a prisoner for forty months, with thirty-four of those months spent in isolation. He entered the war as an atheist, but during his incarceration, he persuaded one of his Japanese guards to loan him a copy of the Bible.

The message of the Bible led to DeShazar's conversion, and he became a strong Christian believer while still a prisoner. Upon his release after the war, he pursued his education and then returned to Japan as a missionary in 1948.

Following the war, DeShazer, the Doolittle Raider who bombed Nagoya, met Japanese Captain Mitsuo Fuchida,[79] who led the first wave of Japanese bombers in the attack on Pearl Harbor, and they became close friends. Fuchida became a Christian in 1950 after reading a tract written about DeShazer, entitled, *I Was a Prisoner of Japan*. After his conversion, Fuchida spent the rest of his life as a minister of the gospel in Asia and the United States. On one occasion, DeShazer and Fuchida preached together as Christian missionaries in Japan. In 1959, DeShazer moved to Nagoya to establish a Christian church in the same city he had bombed in 1942.

The Holy Spirit's work and calling in these two lives, despite the horrors of war, serve as an example of God's grace on display. The fact that two opposing pilots from two of the most famous opposing missions of the war could unite to share the good news of Jesus Christ demonstrates the power of the gospel to bring people together and turn lives around.

The call of God to reach people with His good news transcends every human difficulty and division, including war. He has commissioned us to reach all people everywhere and to do it together. You and I are not mere spectators of the Holy Spirit's work on Earth, but we have been invited to partner with Him to be Jesus' hands and feet in His divine quest for every lost person. Uniting in this mission will change our lives and significantly impact our generation.

> **You and I are not mere spectators of the Holy Spirit's work on Earth, but we have been invited to partner with Him to be Jesus' hands and feet in His divine quest for every lost person.**

Let's revisit the scripture God gave me in my middle-of-the-night prayer meeting. The prophet Habakkuk declared, "For the earth will be filled with the knowledge of the glory of the Lord as the waters cover the sea" (Habakkuk 2:14).

When the Lord spoke to me about a new flood, unlike the one in Noah's day, He told me it would come from three sources. The first one was a fresh, global outpouring of the Holy Spirit like rain from above. The Lord showed me that heaven would answer the heart cry of new generations for an authentic encounter with the Holy Spirit by sending a fresh outpouring of power and glory. Generation Z, in particular, is crying out for authenticity, and they are ready to experience God in tangible and fresh ways.

As this happens, spiritually dry places on the Earth, including difficult-to-reach nations and people, will experience fresh awakenings to God's mercy and grace. No place on the planet will remain exempt from this spiritual deluge.

EVERYONE EVERYWHERE

The second source God revealed to me was the opening of millions of personal wells and internal rivers of witness from believers worldwide. The severe brokenness people are experiencing in the 21st century will open their hearts and lives, so rivers of spiritual life will flow out of them in greater measure than ever before. Christ-followers everywhere will be moved with compassion for the lost and begin to take personal responsibility for the Great Commission, doing their part to reach everyone.

I believe that a genesis of this new flood will be the rekindling of a deep conviction to share the good news of Jesus with others on a personal level.

The World Is Flat was published by Thomas Friedman in 2005. His concept of a flattened world refers to the flattening of hierarchies brought about by technological advancements and globalization, thus creating a more fluid society. Whereas in the past, a person would have to rely on established institutions or gatekeepers to reach large audiences, the interconnectedness of digital platforms today has made it possible for individuals to engage with a global audience on their terms with little-to-no institutional backing. Individuals can now communicate from anywhere to anyone thus creating this "flattened world." Connections and relationships are flowing around the globe.

Anyone, anywhere can now have a platform and reach the world in a split second, as proven by a host of "influencers" who have monetized their reach with great effect. This flattened world, in which every person holds the power to reach into any culture and connect with any person, makes fulfilling the Great Commission completely possible, unlike during any other era in history.

You can now pull out your phone, log on to Instagram or YouTube, begin a live feed, and speak to digital followers worldwide with whatever message you choose. You don't have to work your way to the top of a giant news outlet or media conglomerate—you can go viral from your home with the device in your pocket. We live in a world where every person can become an influencer. Generation Z desires to be one. When asked, one out of four youths and young adults stated they wanted their career to be one of influence.[80] My wife, Lisa, and I have a niece who is a fashion influencer. She does photo shoots in various outfits while on location and uses her perceived expertise to help sell clothing brands. Companies have hired her to use her influence to market their brand, and she is well-paid to do so.

A new era of evangelism is emerging where millions of believers will become gospel influencers—not just on social media platforms, but in the world around them.

The 21st century will be the most opportune time in human history for the fulfillment of the Great Commission. A new era of evangelism is emerging where millions of believers will become gospel influencers—not just on social media platforms, but in the world around them.

In the 20th century, we witnessed a focused anointing on select, individual ministries. God raised amazing leaders like Billy Graham, Oral Roberts, T. L. Osborn, Luis Palau, and Reinhard Bonnke, among many others, who touched millions of lives through their ministries. Conversely, we are now experiencing a distributed anointing. God is now distributing to many, many people this anointing that once rested on a select few.

This is similar to what took place with Moses' leadership of Israel. God told Moses to bring forward seventy of Israel's elders. They were to join Moses at the tent of meeting where God would speak to them and "take some of the power of the Spirit that is on you (Moses) and put it on them" (Numbers 11:25, MSG). The Lord told Moses that these elders would then share the burden of the people with him. God's focused anointing on Moses was distributed to these seventy other leaders, allowing God's work to take on a new dimension.

Tens of thousands of new spirit-empowered leaders are emerging in the world. Some have called them the nameless, faceless generation. They do have names but their names are not known in super wide circles. They are influencers in certain segments, ethnicities, regions, and groups of this flattened world.

They are forming an army of a workforce that God will use during this most significant time in history to complete the greatest task on Earth. In the days ahead, onlookers will not be able to point to just a few Christian mega-personalities as the driving force behind this movement.

Instead, it will be fueled by everyone everywhere, using their influence, which has been afforded to them in a flattened world, to impact the world for Jesus Christ. The Holy Spirit flowing out of each believer will raise the spiritual flood level in every nation on Earth. Just as it happened on the day of Pentecost as God rested His fire on each disciple, He is once again igniting individual believers who will passionately release His glory to their generation.

This new era of anointing is not reserved for full-time ministry professionals such as pastors, evangelists, worship leaders, or missionaries. The promise we read in Joel 2:28, "And afterward, I will pour out my Spirit on all people. Your sons and daughters will prophesy, your old men will dream dreams, your young men will see visions"—reminds us that the Lord will pour out His Spirit upon ALL flesh—everyone!

> **This new era of anointing is not reserved for full-time ministry professionals.**

Beyond doubt, this new era of evangelism requires everyone if we are to reach everyone. We need school teachers with a heart for their students, showing Christ's love and teaching His truth; nurses, doctors, and medical researchers who transform hopeless spaces into places of healing and restoration; artists, performers, writers, and composers who tap into creativity that flows from heaven, transforming culture through their gifting to tell the story of redemption; entrepreneurs and civil servants who labor in their communities to better the lives of their neighbors; men and women in ministry who prioritize personal integrity as paramount while proclaiming the Word of God to this generation with uncompromising boldness; the technician, librarian, farmer, and the rising tide of entrepreneurs in Generation Z. Reaching everyone truly requires everyone—every believer in every field and area of society bearing fruit, operating in the gifts of the Spirit and sharing the gospel with the people around them one person at a time.

The ones who make the greatest impact will be those who wield their influence for God's purpose and go against the status quo to bring heaven to Earth. They will be people who commit to seeing the *one* and building relationships that result in a harvest of salvation. This new era of evangelism will result in all of us carrying the hope and message of Jesus Christ wherever we are and wherever we go.

One clear example of the gospel's transformative power to reach a community, a city, and a nation from a grassroots level is Rome. Today, the city's name is synonymous with the seat of leadership for the Catholic Church, the largest Christian group on Earth. However, during the 1st century, it was a completely different story.

We know that on the day of Pentecost recorded in Acts Chapter 2, Jews and proselytes from Rome were listening to Peter preach. Less than twenty years later, as the apostle Paul was writing a letter to the church that had been established in Rome, we realize that he knew and singled out twenty-six different individuals and five different groups in his salutation (Romans Chapter 16). The church was growing, and the gospel was advancing one person at a time.

As Paul neared the end of his Earthly journey, we read about his imprisonment in Rome as well as his steady leadership and witness for two years culminating in his presentation of the gospel before the rulers of the empire and his martyrdom under Nero.[81] But Christianity continued to spread across the city, and neither persecution, the emperor's wishes, nor prohibitions from the Roman Senate could slow the gospel's advancement.[82] By the year 312 AD, the Roman Emperor Constantine had not only converted to Christianity himself, but he also declared it a legal religion within the Empire one year later through the Edict of Milan.

What started with a few individuals hearing the proclamation of the gospel under the power of the Holy Spirit on the day of Pentecost turned into a movement that swept across not only Rome but the entire Roman empire within a few centuries. Nothing could stop the good news. No legal, cultural, linguistic, ideological, or military barrier would ultimately stand in its way. The gospel of the kingdom was preached, and the government and peace of the King of kings would grow.

Paul, writing to the Romans, penned the following words: "For I am not ashamed of the gospel, because it is the power of God that brings salvation to everyone..." (1:16). Although he didn't see it with his own eyes, he knew it would happen! This good news of Jesus, through the power of His Spirit, has the potential to reach everyone. When the rivers within us break forth in the marketplace of our day, just as they did across the Roman Empire, a new spiritual flood will take place, and we will reach everyone.

ONE BODY, ONE MISSION

The third source for this new flood God impressed upon my heart is the convergence of spiritual streams and movements, joining together in unity to bring a confluence of spiritual power. Where and when believers connect in unity, it will bring an overflow (like a headwater or tailwater effect), and the power of the Holy Spirit will spiritually flood the Earth around these connection points. Movements and streams will converge in our day in new ways, and we will see a great flood of grace.

Unity is powerful! When God's people are united, they can do the impossible. Unity brings supernatural synergy that will allow the church to progress beyond where it has ever been. Synergy is the natural phenomenon that allows the parts to do more together than any one part can do individually and more than they can do when simply added together.

During the years since my visitation from the Lord and the revelation regarding a second flood, I have contemplated and meditated many times on Jesus' prayer in John 17. Jesus offered this prayer to heaven as He concluded His final Passover meal with His disciples before heading to the cross. Philip Melanchthon, Martin Luther's friend, wrote, "There is no voice which has ever been heard, either in heaven or in the Earth, more exalted, more holy, more fruitful, more sublime, than the prayer offered up by the Son of God Himself." A man's heart is revealed in His prayers, and we see the heart of Jesus' revealed to all of us in John Chapter 17. It is by far the most intimate and revealing prayer of Jesus to His Father found anywhere in the New Testament. He certainly foresaw that some of the world's most divided, segregated, isolated people would be those who would believe in Him. Such discord grieved and does grieve His heart. In Jesus' prayer, we find three simple insights I consider critical regarding unity within the church.

First, we must understand that believers' unity must be relational.

Jesus prayed that we would be one as He and the Father are one. He said, "My prayer is not for them alone. I pray also for those who will believe in me through their message, that all of them may be one, Father, just as you are in me, and I am in you. May they also be in us so that the world may believe that you have sent me" (John 17:20–21). This unity among the Godhead—you are in me, and I am in you"—is founded in a relationship flowing from perfect love and submission.

I believe the unprecedented unity we will experience in the days ahead will be an ever-increasing, relational unity birthed and bathed in love and submission to one another. We are witnessing a new era of relational unity in the 21st century. Individuals and constituted groups are rising above their traditional divisions to love and mutually submit to one another, humble themselves, and build relational bonds that tie the worldwide body of Christ together.

The second insight from Jesus' prayer is that, while unity is relational in scope, it must be missional in intent.

Jesus prayed that the world would believe God had sent Him because of our unity: "I in them and you in me—so that they may be brought to complete unity. Then the world will know that you sent me and have loved them even as you have loved me" (John 17:23). Relating to one another in love is of utmost importance, yet God has something more in mind than just embracing unity for the sake of unity.

After years of experience convening Christian leaders, I have discovered that relational networks deteriorate unless they have a united mission. Relationships deepen when our unity is focused on a common missional purpose, and the kingdom of God advances. We've seen discord in the church because the enemy hates this unity that threatens his kingdom of darkness. When we come together, the potential is massive.

Like a laser, unity among believers allows the message of Christ to penetrate hard-to-reach people groups while creating a multiplication effect for our efforts. Working together releases God's presence to do what one of us working alone could never do. This supernatural synergy not only brings the power of two together, but it also multiplies the effect beyond the ability of the united parties. Something supernatural happens in unity: God is pleased, and His blessing on united effort produces the supernatural synergy that allows us to accomplish more than we ever dreamed possible.

"How good and pleasant it is when God's people live together in unity! It is like precious oil poured on the head, running down on the beard, running down on Aaron's beard, down on the collar of his robe. It is as if the dew of Hermon were falling on Mount Zion. For there the LORD bestows his blessing, even life forevermore" (Psalms 133:1–3).

Unity is like the consecration oil that was poured upon Aaron to install him in the office of the high priest (see Exodus 30:22–30). When we dwell in harmony with our brothers and sisters, the fragrance of the Holy Spirit increases upon us, strategically equipping us for God's work. We need God's oil to set us in place for effectiveness in our mission. When God's people unite, supernatural power and energy are released.

I learned about this dynamic of synergy firsthand as a child. My grandfather loved horses, mules, donkeys, ponies—anything of the equine variety. Periodically, he would take me to horse and pony "Pullins." These were events where teams of horses or ponies were tested for their strength and endurance in pulling heavy loads.

A sleigh filled with concrete blocks was used as the testing instrument, and depending on the number of blocks successfully transported, the animal's proficiency was demonstrated. At times, horses were tested for their strength although they usually pulled in teams. We learned the lesson of synergy by observing a horse or its teammate pulling several hundred pounds individually. This was considered their maximum, individual ability. However, when those same two horses pulled together, they would move much more than their individual maximums combined.

In other words, their ability was increased significantly by working together. Corporately, they were stronger than they were individually.

Supernatural synergy happens when the people of God work in tandem and pull together toward God's purpose. This principle is demonstrated in Scripture: "Five of you will chase a hundred, and a hundred of you will chase ten thousand, and your enemies will fall by the sword before you" (Leviticus. 26:8). "How could one man chase a thousand, or two put ten thousand to flight, unless their Rock had sold them, unless the LORD had given them up?" (Deuteronomy 32:30).

We should not be surprised when we consider the way Jesus sent out His disciples. He sent them in pairs, two by two. He understood the dynamic power of supernatural synergy at play and valued their increased effectiveness far more than potential geographical coverage. To reach their potential, they needed one another! As we consider the Great Commission, the words of Steve Moore from Missio Nexus are very appropriate: "The Great Commission is too big for anyone to accomplish alone and too important not to try to do together."[83]

The third insight from Jesus' prayer is that true unity can only happen in an environment filled with God's presence and glory: "I have given them the glory that you gave me, that they may be one as we are one" (John 17:22).

We hear much about relational unity and shared mission, but we often omit this critical element to fulfilling Jesus' prayer. Simply put, "God's glory is the rest of the story." When God is at work, He brings us together in ways we could never forge by human activity alone.

Without His presence and the work of the Holy Spirit, our attempts at unity are futile and limited to human ingenuity. In our horizontal efforts to relate and share in the mission, we will experience frustration, and our witness will be limited without the vertical connection with heaven required to experience unity.

Christian hypocrisy concerning loving one another is one of the greatest struggles the unbeliever must overcome to believe the gospel. It's time to be united!

As we lift our eyes to the burgeoning harvest before us, we must realize unity is needed now more than ever. The good news of Jesus is worth uniting for. If Jesus and the sharing of His gospel could bring together Jacob DeShazer and Mitsuo Fuchida, two opposing enemies during one of the most significant wars in history, surely this good news can unite us across our denominational differences.

The good news of Jesus is worth uniting for.

If we are willing to unite together, we can form a net to bring in the largest catch of human beings in the history of the world. No one ministry, denomination, or person could ever reach eight billion people. I believe God is calling us to live "Great Commandment lifestyles" and fulfill the Great Commission in our day as we witness a flood of His glory until no dry place remains on Earth. The Great Commission is possible, but it is going to take everyone!

2033!

I've been deeply encouraged as I witness various movements and denominations within the church coming together, united in the mission to reach everyone with the gospel by 2033. In December 2022, I gathered with multiple leaders, movement heads, and ecumenical groups in New York City to draft what we are calling "2033: A Call to the Global Church for a Decade of Great Commission Effort." We believe that the decade leading to 2033 will be one of unprecedented evangelism through which everyone on Earth can be reached with the good news. This document serves as a common thread to unite movements in their efforts to fulfill the Great Commission and align our focus.[84]

We believe that the decade leading to 2033 will be one of unprecedented evangelism through which everyone on Earth can be reached with the good news.

In 2033, the church will celebrate the 2,000-year anniversary of Christ's crucifixion, resurrection, ascension, and the outpouring of the Holy Spirit on the day of Pentecost. In 2013, when the Empowered21 Global

Council gathered to write the network's vision, we oscillated between 2030 and 2033 to benchmark this moment in history, finally landing in 2033. God's people in this decade leading to 2033 will be strategic and dynamically stable unlike any before.

A new era of evangelism is dawning.

A new era of evangelism is dawning. God is realigning our focus, hearts, and efforts to reach the world one person at a time. This is the strategy God has given us for fulfilling the Great Commission. It starts with people like you and me. In this next decade, let's join together for a united purpose and reach every single person on Earth through the power of the Holy Spirit with the message of Jesus Christ!

CONCLUSION

When the scarred feet of Jesus finally disappeared out of sight, the disciples were left standing in awe on the Mount of Olives. Their resurrected Master and Savior had just ascended into the heavens. They had been eyewitnesses to the greatest life and ministry of all time. Their lives and the world would never be the same. Jesus had finished His Earthly ministry, and now their turn had come.

Their marching orders were clear: First, they were to return to Jerusalem and wait for the Father's promised Holy Spirit. Afterward, they were to go into all nations, taking the amazing news of Jesus' resurrection to one and all. Everyone in their generation—Jew and Gentile alike—deserved to hear this life-changing message and have an authentic encounter with the resurrected Jesus.

The disciples obeyed and turned their world upside down for Christ. People everywhere, in all walks of life, from every ethnicity and a multitude of religious backgrounds would hear and experience the good news. They ". . . went everywhere preaching, the Master working right with them, validating the Message with indisputable evidence" (Mark 16:20, MSG). They filled Jerusalem with this message and, within decades, filled the Roman world with the knowledge of the glory of the Lord.

Now, almost two thousand years since Jesus' resurrection and the giving of the Great Commission, we have our turn. The baton of the good news is in our hands, and the road extends before us.

The baton of the good news is in our hands.

The world population is larger than it has ever been, and our tools for sharing the knowledge of God's glory are also greater than ever. Our opportunity is unprecedented, and we are being called to make an unprecedented effort to reach every person on Earth in our generation.

The Power of One has been written to encourage you and today's church to personalize the Great Commission afresh and refocus on the significance of reaching every individual. The road to paradise is narrow. The doorway to eternal fellowship with God is Jesus, Himself. Only in having a personal relationship with Him can anyone be saved. People go to heaven one person at a time, not in groups or families. We are commissioned to share God's good news with everyONE because His will is that not ONE should perish.

Our assignment can be completed! Just consider if one person shared the good news with another person; the next day those two people shared the good news with two other people; then those four shared the gospel with four others, and . . . Finishing the task to share the amazing news of Jesus with every person on Earth would only require thirty-three days! Even if every believer just shared the good news with one new person each week, it would take less than thirty-three weeks (eight months) to reach everyone on Earth.

Obviously, this is oversimplified, but when you add the power of technology, television networks, social media, movies, print media, digital connections, telephone capabilities, AI, the Metaverse, and the tools yet to be developed, the opportunities for sharing Jesus are unlike any time in history.

The real question is: *Will* we DO IT?

On the two thousandth anniversary of Jesus' death on the cross, resurrection, and ascension, will we place at His feet the greatest effort toward fulfilling the Great Commission in Christian history? Will we synergize our Spirit-empowered ministries to reach everyone for Christ in our generation? I believe we can, and we will, but each one of us is key. Hopefully, *The Power of One* has helped us recognize that within every convert, a huge capacity exists for good. Heaven rejoices when a name is written in the Lamb's Book of Life, and Earth is impacted by the release of their kingdom potential. Like the demoniac of Gadara, the woman at the well, the repentant thief on the cross, the Ethiopian Eunuch, Cornelius, the Philippian jailer, the apostle Paul, and thousands of others throughout history, one person can make a profound difference for Christ.

What about you? What difference will your life make?

What is the kingdom potential inside of you?

Yes, the task is big, and no one individual can do it all. Yet, all of us can do something.

American author, Edward Everett Hale wrote:

I am only one,

But still, I am one,

I cannot do everything,

But still, I can do something;

And because I cannot do everything,

I will not refuse to do something that I can do.

You are only one, but you are one, and through the Holy Spirit's empowerment, the potential for kingdom impact within you is enormous. Commit today that you will never refuse to do what you can do. When you make an effort to reach others, you will be amazed by the potential that is released. God will multiply your efforts through His power, and generations will be affected positively as you engage. My prayer for you is that these will be the most exciting days of your life as you unite with millions of other believers in pursuing the greatest task ever given. By God's grace, your life will demonstrate to the world . . . **The Power of ⦿N☰.**

You are only one, but you are one, and through the Holy Spirit's empowerment, the potential for kingdom impact within you is enormous.

ENDNOTES

INTRODUCTION

1   The Story Pastor Neil Smith referenced to Dr. Wilson is a widely circulated story from Reinhard Bonnke's ministry amongst evangelists and missions. One example can be found here: https://www.youtube.com/watch?v=UolKuW7zWW0

CHAPTER 1

2   Martin, K. (12 Oct. 2020). *Private First Class Desmond Thomas Doss Medal of Honor.* The National WWII Museum. www.nationalww2museum.org/war/articles/private-first-class-desmond-thomas-doss-medal-of-honor

3   Screen Zone. (2017, February 21). *Hacksaw Ridge "Desmond Doss Life And Speech"* [Video]. YouTube. https://www.youtube.com/watch?v=R8pPPItJlJs

4   Admin. (2020, May 5). *Desmond T. Doss Remembered 75 Years After Heroic Actions in WWII.* Desmond T. Doss Christian . Academy. http://www.desmondtdoss.org/desmond-t-doss-remembered-75-years-after-heroic-actions-in-wwii/

5   Lewis, C. S. (1962). Perelandra (1st ed.). Pan.

6   United Nations (2022, November 1). *UN DESA Policy Brief
         No. 140: A World of 8 Billion.* Department of Economic and
         Social Affairs. Retrieved May 23, 2023, from https://www.
         un.org/en/dhttps://www.un.org/development/desa/dpad/
         publication/un-desa-policy-brief-no-140-a-world-of-8-
         billion/#:~:text=Department%20of%20Economic%20and%20
         Social%20Affairsayof8billion

7   Worldometer. (2023). *World Population Clock.* Worldometers.
         https://www.worldometers.info/world-population/

8   Hackett, C., & McClendon, D. (2017, April 5). *Christians
         remain world's largest religious group, but they are declining in
         Europe.* Pew Research Center. https://www.pewresearch.org/
         short-reads/2017/04/05/christians-remain-worlds-largest-
         religious-group-but-they-are-declining-in-europe/

9   *"Jefferson is in every view less dangerous than Burr": Hamilton
         on the election of 1800.* (n.d.) Gilder Lehrman Institute
         of American History. https://www.gilderlehrman.
         org/history-resources/spotlight-primary-source/
         jefferson-every-view-less-dangerous-burr-hamilton

10   *Birth of the Third Republic, 1875.* (2016, November 22). Palace
         of Versailles. https://en.chateauversailles.fr/discover/history/
         key-dates/birth-third-republic-1875

11   Lehmann-Haupt, H. E. (2018). *Johannes Gutenberg* | Printing
         Press, Facts, & Biography. In Encyclopædia Britannica.
         https://www.britannica.com/biography/Johannes-Gutenberg

12   *The Holocaust.* (2023). The National WWII Museum | New Orleans; The National WWII Museum. https://www. nationalww2museum.org/war/articles/holocaust

13   History.com Editors. (n.d.). *Rosa Parks: Bus Boycott, Civil Rights & Facts.* History.com. https://www.history.com/topics/ black-history/rosa-parks#

14   Bauer, P. (2019). *Norma McCorvey* | Biography & Facts. In Encyclopædia Britannica. https://www.britannica.com/ biography/Norma-McCorvey

15   *Abortions United States Data and Trends.* (n.d.). https://nrlc. org/uploads/factsheets/FS01AbortionintheUS.pdf

16   Liptak, A. (2022, June 24). *In 6-to-3 Ruling, Supreme Court Ends Nearly 50 Years of Abortion Rights.* The New York Times. https://www.nytimes.com/2022/06/24/us/roe-wade-overturned-supreme-court.html

17   Aksenov, P. (2013, September 26). *Stanislav Petrov: The man who may have saved the world.* BBC News. https://www.bbc. com/news/world-europe-24280831

CHAPTER 2

18   *David Brainerd* | American missionary | Britannica. (n.d.). www.britannica.com. https://www.britannica.com/biography/ David-Brainerd

19   Piper, J. (1991, July 1). *For Single Men and Women (and the Rest of Us)*. Desiring God. https://www.desiringgod.org/articles/for-single-men-and-women-and-the-rest-of-us

20   *Who Was John Geddie?* (n.d.). Ligonier Ministries. Retrieved May 22, 2023, from https://www.ligonier.org/learn/articles/missionary-john-geddie

21   *No Heathens* | Bible.org. (n.d.). Bible.org. Retrieved May 22, 2023, from https://bible.org/illustration/no-heathens

22   *William Booth.* (n.d.). The Salvation Army International Heritage Center. https://www2.calmview.co.uk/SalvationArmy/CalmView/Record.aspx?src=CalmView.Catalog&id=CC%2f3&pos=2

23   (2020, July 2). *The Best 18 Quotes from William Booth.* Caring Magazine. https://caringmagazine.org/the-best-18-quotes-from-william-booth/

24   Further reading: Elliot, E. (2015). *Through Gates of Splendor.* Hendrickson Publishers. Saint, S. (2005). *End of the Spear: A True Story.* Tyndale House Publishers.

25   Petersen, M., & Borghy, B. (2019, March 19). *William Cameron "Uncle Cam" Townsend (1896–1982).* Encyclopedia of Arkansas. https://encyclopediaofarkansas.net/entries/william-cameron-uncle-cam-townsend-4453/

26   *William Cameron Townsend. (n.d.).* The Traveling Team. Retrieved May 24, 2023, from https://www.thetravelingteam. org/articles/william-cameron-townsend

27   Morgan, R. J. (1998). *From This Verse.*

28   ibid.

CHAPTER 3

29   Vernon, J. L. (2017, June 12). *Understanding the Butterfly Effect.* American Scientist. https://www.americanscientist.org/article/ understanding-the-butterfly-effect

30   *The Butterfly Effect - Why What You Do Matters* | Andy Andrews | TEDxRiverOaks. (n.d.). YouTube. https://www. youtube.com/watch?v=NRgmm4xyyU0

31   See Biblical Account in Mark 5.

32   *Divorce in the Bible.* (n.d.). My Jewish Learning. https://www. myjewishlearning.com/article/divorce-in-the-bible/

33   See Biblical Account in Acts 8:26-40.

34   Zurlo, G.A. *Who Owns Global Christianity?* (2019, December 11). Gordon Conwell. https://www.gordonconwell.edu/blog/ who-owns-global-christianity/

CHAPTER 4

35   *Illuminations - Translating God's Word for All.* (n.d.). Illuminations.bible. Retrieved April 27, 2023, from https://illuminations.bible/about

36   Morgan, R. J. (1998). *From This Verse.*

37   *One Person at a Time.* (September 23, 2016). Wycliffe Bible Translators. https://www.wycliffe.org/blog/featured/one-person-at-a-time

38   *Who is Edward Kimball?* (July 28, 2015.). NewLife Christian Fellowship: Wethersfield, CT. Retrieved May 22, 2023, from https://www.newlife-ct.org/the-newlife-blog/post/who-is-edward-kimball

39   *Billy Graham's Life & Ministry By the Numbers.* (2018, February 21). Lifeway Research. https://research.lifeway.com/2018/02/21/billy-grahams-life-ministry-by-the-numbers/

40   Douthat, R. (2014, March 15). Opinion: *The Age of Individualism.* The New York Times. https://www.nytimes.com/2014/03/16/opinion/sunday/douthat-the-age-of-individualism.html

41   Santos, H. C., Varnum, M. E. W., & Grossmann, I. (2017). *Global Increases in Individualism.* Psychological Science, 28(9), 1228–1239. https://doi.org/10.1177/095679761770062

42   Spitznagel, E. (2020, January 26). *Generation Z is bigger than millennials — and they're out to change the world.* New York

Post. https://nypost.com/2020/01/25/generation-z-is-bigger-than-millennials-and-theyre-out-to-change-the-world/

43   McKnight, K. *Gen Z and the challenges of the most individualistic generation yet.* (2018, December 7). Illume Network. https://illumestories.com/gen-z-and-the-challenges-of-the-most-individualistic-generation-yet/#:~:text=Individualism%20is%20on%20a%20continual

44   Pruitt, S. (2017, September 21). 10 *Characteristics of Generation Z.* ChurchLeaders. https://churchleaders.com/outreach-missions/outreach-missions-articles/310160-10-characteristics-generation-z-shane-pruitt.html

45   The Annie E. Casey Foundation. (2021, February 14). *Social Issues That Matter to Generation Z.* The Annie E. Casey Foundation. https://www.aecf.org/blog/generation-z-social-issues

46   Joshua Project. Joshuaproject.net. https://joshuaproject.net/

47   *YouVersion Bible App celebrates 10th anniversary.* (2018, July 9). YouVersion. https://www.youversion.com/press/youversion-bible-app-celebrates-10th-anniversary/

48   YouVersion Bible App. https://www.youversion.com/the-bible-app

49   Christa. (2022, May 28). *"The Chosen Series" Reached Over 400 Million Views Worldwide.* God TV News. https://godtv.com/the-chosen-series-400-million-views-worldwide/

50 *The Chosen Subtitled Languages and Dubbed Audio.* (2023, January 5). Angel Studios. https://www.angel.com/blog/the-chosen/posts/the-chosen-subtitles-and-languages

51 Steinbuch, Y. (2021, February 11). *Every COVID-19 particle on Earth could fit in Coke can: scientist says.* New York Post. https://nypost.com/2021/02/11/every-covid-19-particle-on-earth-could-fit-in-coke-can-scientist/

52 theworldcounts.com. Retrieved May 23, 2023, from https://www.theworldcounts.com/challenges/planet-earth/state-of-the-planet/world-population-clock-live

53 Bouwsma, W. J. (2018). *John Calvin* | French theologian. In Encyclopædia Britannica. https://www.britannica.com/biography/John-Calvin

54 Calvin, J., 1960. *Institutes of the Christian Religion.* 1st ed. Philadelphia: The Westminster Press, p.1960.

55 *Life expectancy in the USA, 1900-98.* (2019). Berkeley.edu. https://u.demog.berkeley.edu/~andrew/1918/figure2.html

CHAPTER 5

56 CDC. (2019). *FastStats - life expectancy.* Centers for Disease Control and Prevention. https://www.cdc.gov/nchs/fastats/life-expectancy.html

57 History.com Editors. (2009, November 6). *Wright Brothers.* History.com; A&E Television Networks. https://www.history. com/topics/inventions/wright-brothers

58 Clark, C. (n.d.). *This incredible animation shows every airline flight in the world over a 24 hour period.* Business Insider. https://www.businessinsider.com/video-shows-every-airline-flight-in-the-world-over-a-24-hour-period-2016-3

59 Stephens, M. (2020). *History of Television - Mitchell Stephens.* Nyu.edu; Grolier Encyclopedia. https://stephens.hosting.nyu. edu/History%20of%20Television%20page.html

60 Young, A., Harrington, J. (2020, September 6) World History: *These are among the most important global events to happen annually since 1920.* usatoday.com. https://www.usatoday.com/ story/money/2020/09/06/the-worlds-most-important-event-every-year-since-1920/113604790/

61 Goetsch, A. (2005, May 2) The Evolution of GPS. Illumin.usc. edu. https://illumin.usc.edu/the-evolution-of-gps/

62 Young, A. Harrington, J. (2020, September 6) World History: *These are among the most important global events to happen annually since 1920.* usatoday.com. https://www.usatoday.com/ story/money/2020/09/06/the-worlds-most-important-event-every-year-since-1920/113604790/

63 ibid.

64 ibid.

65   Bhandari, K, S. (2022, June 20) Social Media Day: *The Evolution of Virtual Platforms.* entrepreneur.com. https://www.entrepreneur.com/en-in/social-media/ social-media-day-the-evolution-of-virtual-platforms/430535

66   Young, A., Harrington, J. (2020, September 6) World History: *These are among the most important global events to happen annually since 1920. usatoday.com.* https://www.usatoday.com/ story/money/2020/09/06/the-worlds-most-important-event-every-year-since-1920/113604790/

67   ibid.

68   ibid.

69   Meta. (2021, October 28) *Introducing Meta: A Social Technology Company.* about.fb.com. https://about.fb.com/news/2021/10/ facebook-company-is-now-meta/#:~:text=Today%20at%20 Connect%202021%2C%20CEO,find%20communities%20 and%20grow%20businesses

70   DeGeurin, M. *ChatGPT Creator Tells Congress AI Text Is Photoshop on Steroids.* (2023, May 16). Gizmodo. https:// gizmodo.com/chatgpt-ai-openai-sam-altman-congress-watch-hearing-1850440738

71   Ray, A. *Human knowledge is doubling every 12 hours.* (n.d.). www.linkedin.com. Retrieved May 22, 2023, from https://www.linkedin.com/pulse/

human-knowledge-doubling-every-12-hours-amitabh-
ray#:~:text= Two%20things%20are%20happening%20at

72   *Gen Z is leading a new era of salary transparency.* (n.d.).
Handshake. https://joinhandshake.com/network-trends/
gen-z-salary-transparency/

73   *William Carey.* (2008, August 8). Christian History |
Learn the History of Christianity & the Church; Christian
History. https://www.christianitytoday.com/history/people/
missionaries/william-carey.html

74   Gordon, E. B. (1896). *Adoniram Judson Gordon.*

CHAPTER 6

75   Citino, R. (2021, November 11). *Pearl Harbor Attack,
December 7, 1941.* The National WWII Museum | New
Orleans. https://www.nationalww2museum.org/war/topics/
pearl-harbor-december-7-1941

76   Franklin D. Roosevelt Presidential Library and Museum.
(2016). *FDR Biography.* FDR Presidential Library &
Museum. Fdrlibrary.org. https://www.fdrlibrary.org/
fdr-biography

77   Vergun, D., DOD News. (2020, April 18). *Doolittle
Raid on Japan 78 Years Ago Buoyed American Spirits.*
U.S. Department of Defense. https://www.defense.

gov/News/Feature-Stories/story/Article/2148287/
doolittle-raid-on-japan-78-years-ago-buoyed-american-spirits/

78   *Deshazer.* (n.d.). Children of the Doolittle Raiders. Retrieved
      May 23, 2023, from https://www.childrenofthedoolittleraiders.
      com/crew-members/team-members/deshazer/

79   *Mitsuo Fuchida: from Pearl Harbor attacker to Christian
      evangelist* | Christian History Magazine. (n.d.). Christian
      History Institute. https://christianhistoryinstitute.org/
      magazine/article/mitsuo-fuchida-christian-evangelist

80   Suciu, P. (n.d.). *Young People Want To Be Influencers
      Even As Older Americans Say It Isn't A Real Job!* Forbes.
      Retrieved May 22, 2023, from https://www.forbes.com/
      sites/petersuciu/2022/10/20/young-people-want-to-be-
      influencers-even-as-older-americans-say-it-isnt-a-real-
      job/?sh=69a65b835f04

81   Eusebius (1926). *The Ecclesiastical History.* William
      Heinemann.

82   Cairns, E. E. (1980). *Christianity through the centuries.*
      Zondervan Pub. House.

83   Moore, S. (2017). *The Top 10 Leadership Conversations in the
      Bible.*

84   For more information or to sign the Everyone 2033
      Commitment go to https://2033.earth/